Paramahamsa
Nithyananda

Published by:
eNPublishers
Nithyananda Mission, Bidadi Ashram,
Nithyanandapuri, Kallugopahalli,
Off Mysore Road, Bidadi,
Bangalore District - 562 109.
Karnataka, INDIA
URL: www.nithyananda.org, www.enpublishers.com
Email: eNPublishers@nithyananda.org

*Discourses delivered to Swamis and Ananda Samajis
of the Nithyananda Order all over the world.*

Open the door... let the breeze in!
tools for joyful living

Paramahamsa
Nithyananda

CONTENTS

EMPTY YOURSELF!
PREPARING TO RECEIVE LIFE

EMPTY YOURSELF!
PREPARING TO RECEIVE LIFE

A popular Zen story goes like this:

> One day, a famous professor approached the great Zen master Nansen to seek clarification on some philosophical matters. The master lived in a cottage in the forest, and the professor had to walk a long way to meet him.
> When he reached the cottage, the master was boiling water for making tea.
> The professor's head was full of questions for Nansen, and he started asking them right away.
> Wait, said the master, let us have tea first.
> But the professor was impatient. Not only did he want his questions answered, he also wanted to show off his knowledge to Nansen. So while Nansen brewed the tea, he continued to talk about this theory and that philosophy, asking Nansen's opinion and giving his own.
> Finally Nansen finished making the tea. He brought the teapot and two empty cups, and set down one cup before the professor.
> When will you answer my questions, master? There is so much I have to learn from you! exclaimed the professor politely.
> In reply, Nansen started silently pouring the tea into the professor's cup. He poured and poured, till the cup was overflowing. Still he continued to pour.
> Zen masters are known to be a bit crazy, but this was too much!
> What are you doing? Can't you see that this cup can't hold any more tea? It is already full! cried the professor in amazement.
> Nansen smiled and asked, Is that so? Then how come _you_ haven't emptied _your_ cup?

9

Zen masters usually talk in riddles, but the professor was an intelligent man, and he understood.

He himself was the cup that Nansen was talking about! He was already so full of ideas, of his borrowed philosophies and acquired knowledge, that there was no way Nansen could have taught him anything. He had no space left for learning anything new!

Before you can learn anything new, you need to first empty your cup.

What did the master mean by emptying your cup?

We all go through life carrying a whole lot of baggage. Physical baggage we can see and understand - all the articles we possess, our homes, our money, our certificates.

If I tell you, Empty your life of all this baggage, at least you would know what I am talking about.

But what about all the baggage that you don't even realize you're carrying inside?

All of us are brimming over with our ideas and philosophies of life.

We have our preconceived notions on every subject under the sun. We have already come to a conclusion as to what will work for us, and what won't.

We have solutions for every problem in the world - except our own, though we will never admit that!

In addition to that, we all have our share of fears and memories that influence how we think, how we learn, how we live, how we act.

In other words, we have all managed to become so full of ourselves that there is NO MORE SPACE for anything new!

When you read this, it naturally means you are looking to learn something new. Of course, if you are reading it out of mere curiosity, if you are certain that you already know all that you need to know, that's perfectly alright. You can go ahead and read it, just as you are.

But if you are looking to learn something, gain something from the time you spend with me, I suggest to you:

Empty your cup.

Another small story. It tells you about the attitude of the true learner!

A brilliant mathematician called Ouspensky once approached the philosopher Gurdjieff to learn from him. Just like with the professor and the Zen master, Ouspensky wanted to clear some doubts from Gurdjieff.

Always, only the most intelligent and successful people have all these doubts! Naturally, when a man is starving, he has no time or inclination to think about spirituality. Only when you have already filled your cup with wealth, with knowledge, with success, do you realise that something is still missing, some flavour is missing. Only then do you take the step towards spirituality.

When Ouspensky approached Gurdjieff, he was already a well-known mathematician. He had done path breaking work in mathematics. Naturally, he had the pride of knowledge. At that time, Gurdjieff was hardly known to the public.

Still, Ouspensky was intelligent enough to realize that there was something in Gurdjieff, something that he might learn from him.

So he approached Gurdjieff and told him, Master, I think that there is a lot that I can learn from you in many areas. Will you teach me?

Certainly, said Gurdjieff. He had a different way of tackling the learner; not like the Zen master!

He simply said, Before I start, why don't you first make a list of all the subjects which you already know about? Then we need not waste time discussing those subjects, and I can concentrate on the other subjects which you need to learn.

So Ouspensky went into the next room with a paper and pencil, and sat down to make the list.

Ouspensky writes later in his memoirs:

Sitting there, for the first time, I realized that I couldn't put a single thing on my list! Unless I was completely sure of a subject, I could not write down that name on the list. There was no way to get past Gurdjieff, he was too wise. If I mentioned a subject and he questioned me about it, I may not be able to answer.

11

The more I thought about it, the more I realized that I knew no subject totally, deeply, truly! For the first time in my life, I realized that I knew nothing. After forty-five minutes, Ouspensky returned to Gurdjieff. Without a word, he placed the blank paper at Gurdjieff's feet. Gurdjieff embraced Ouspensky with a smile, saying, At last, it seems that you have begun knowing...!

To know that you don't know is the beginning of wisdom! When you know that you don't know, you at least know that you don't know. You at least know that much. When you don't know that you don't know, you don't even know that you don't know! That's where all the trouble lies.

* * * * *

When I say empty, emptiness itself is of two kinds:
One is negative, passive emptiness - emptiness that you experience, but cannot control; emptiness that leaves you feeling depleted in some way, the feeling of something lacking. Then there is positive, happy, active emptiness. It is the emptiness that results when you've thrown out everything from your life which is not absolutely essential.
It is something like the difference between loneliness and aloneness!
The first kind of emptiness, you have all experienced at some point in time. In fact, for many people, this is a permanent state of affairs.
This kind of emptiness is precisely what society, what the media strikes at. It is the easiest way to penetrate into you, because it is your weakest spot. Practically every brand in the market works on this principle: making you feel that your life is in some way less rich, in some way incomplete and empty, if you don't own their product!

In marketing terminology, there is a phrase called creating a need. Imagine! Their job is to first create a need that you don't feel right now, and then plug in their product to fill that need.

What professionals do in a formal manner, society does informally. You are made to feel empty if you don't possess the right kind of husband or wife, if you don't have the required number of children, if you don't have a certain kind of job.

> In the Shiva Purana, there is the story of Shiva and the Brahma Kapala. The Brahma Kapala was a skull that Shiva used as a begging bowl, when he was wandering in the guise of a mendicant. The strange thing about the Brahma Kapala was, whatever alms people put into it would promptly be swallowed by the bowl itself! No matter how hard Shiva tried to fill it, the bowl always remained empty.

This Brahma Kapala is inside all of us.

All our lives we keep trying to fill the emptiness inside us. We try to fill it with wealth, with knowledge, with relationships.

Like a black hole, it swallows all that we throw into it. And foolishly, we keep on throwing more and more in, we invest more and more in filling our emptiness.

But finally, even when we are overflowing with success, we feel that something is missing.

When I was a wandering monk in Bengal, I once came across a peanut seller on the roadside. She used a small wicker basket as her measure. When a customer came, she would heap peanuts high in the basket and spill it out into the customer's bag. But strangely, when the peanuts fell into the bag, the quantity seemed to magically decrease! It took me a while to figure out her trick - the basket she used had a false bottom! So even though the basket looked full from the outside, it was actually half empty inside.

I wonder how many customers she played this trick on, before getting caught!

If you notice, Nansen and Gurdjieff used two radically opposite techniques with their disciples. Nansen showed the professor that he was already too full inside. Gurdjieff put Ouspensky in touch with the emptiness inside himself.

But essentially, both of them were saying the same thing, because the fullness and emptiness are essentially the same! Like the peanut-seller, we only create a false sense of fullness to cover up for the emptiness inside.

That's why the master has a dual task.

First, I have to remove all the garbage you have collected inside you, over the years.

Then, I have to create the right kind of emptiness inside you, a positive emptiness.

I have to make you ready to receive.

It is not easy to become empty!

To become empty is the most frightening thing in the world.

Your ego thrives on your fullness. It will continue to cling to everything that gives you the feeling of being somebody. How can you become nobody? Your ego simply cannot tolerate it!

To be empty of the self is the greatest of miracles.

When I say, empty your cup, I am not asking you to throw out all the knowledge you have accumulated. I am not putting down the value of all that you have learnt. Certainly, knowledge has a role in your life. For the kind of life you have been leading, knowledge is essential.

But now you are entering a different zone.

What I am asking you to do, is to put aside your habits, your prejudices, your preconceived ideas.

I am asking you to become sensitive, to become receptive.

I don't ask you to believe or disbelieve.

Just be completely open, just see with open eyes.

Every moment will be transformed into an opportunity for learning.

THE SUN IN A JAR
EXPLORE YOUR TRUE POTENTIAL

THE SUN IN A JAR
EXPLORE YOUR TRUE POTENTIAL

In March 2004, an Indian-born scientist, Dr. Rusi Taleyarkhan, announced an astonishing breakthrough in nuclear fusion - which he called Making the Sun in a Jar.

In this desktop experiment, using the most basic equipment, the scientist and his team managed to achieve nuclear fusion, and generate energy comparable to what is created in the sun! It is as unbelievable as 'making' the sun in a jar, but it has happened.

We shouldn't be surprised at this; we are each of us nothing but a sun in a jar!

Squeezed into the volume of a five or six-foot body, living in the confines of three dimensions, you are simply not aware of your own potential - physical, mental or spiritual.

You are a miracle of super intelligence that technology can never hope to create.

Your body is composed of 50 trillion cells functioning in perfect harmony.

Your brain is a system of ten thousand million neurons transmitting information at 200 miles an hour.

Your eyes can distinguish 16 million shades of colour. Every day, without instructions and without rest, your heart pumps several litres of blood to every corner of your body. Your DNA carries the intelligence that tells every cell whether it should grow into a muscle or blood or skin.

And still you wonder, Will my stomach upset take care of itself, or should I visit the doctor?

Neuroscientists have shown that the average man doesn't use more than 8-12% of his brain. Even an Einstein or Leonardo Da Vinci did not use more than 20-25% of his brain-power!

No IQ test can measure the actual capacity of your brain. IQ tests measure only conscious processes, and much of your mental activity is unconscious. Your unconscious mind stores enormous amounts of information that you don't even know you know!

For instance, can you tell if an earthquake is going to occur in the next ten days?

Can you remember the exact words of a conversation that happened last week?

Can you even tell how many trees or lamp-posts you passed on your way to work this morning?

Of course not!

But under hypnosis, or under circumstances when your unconscious is awakened, you will be able to tell precisely. Almost everybody will be able to tell!

We have focused so hard on developing our conscious mind that we have lost touch with our unconscious. We have lost our mystical contact with the cosmos, with the collective wisdom of the cosmos that has been stored in our unconscious. The 20th century psychologist Carl Jung suggested the term collective consciousness to describe this.

Whether you know it or not, whether you believe it or not, whether you accept it or not, we are linked to every single thing in the universe. Like spokes on a wheel, we only appear to have separate identities on the surface, but as we go deeper, we realize that the center is one.

An eye-opening experiment has been conducted by Cleve Backster, an interrogation specialist with CIA.

As a trial to check the reaction of plants to different electrical stimuli, Backster connected a potted plant in his office to a lie-detector. This is a machine which registers electrical changes in our bodies on a graph (just like an ECG registers changes in our cardiac activity).

When the plant didn't show any response to weak stimuli, Backster decided to try burning one of its leaves.

At the exact moment when that thought arose in his mind, he found that the plant registered a shocking response on the graph!

Astonished, Backster repeated this with other plants and found that not only the plant he was thinking of harming, but all the plants in the room registered this response in different degrees! Later, he discovered that the plants were sensitive to the sound of his voice, and even to his presence in the room.

This experiment proved something even more miraculous than telepathy which is the transmission of information from one human brain to another through an unknown form of communication.

It showed that every cell has the ability to reach out and communicate with every other cell, whether plant or human. A cell that is about to die is able to communicate its fear to other cells, and they can 'feel' sympathy for it! Every cell carries intelligence...and compassion. Cosmic wisdom is available to all who ask for it.

Every one of us has experienced some moments of deep communion, at some time in our life.

It may have been a rare experience of nature's beauty, or deep love, or a moment of prayer; at some time we have all felt that we are more than just our body, that we share a deep connection with all of Existence. Once we break the barriers of our ego, it will be easy to realize this.

The ego perceives everything as separate from itself. That's why the ego finds the world such a terrifying place! We are so afraid to take the leap of understanding, so we live and die without discovering our true potential.

Have you heard the story of the blind man and the stick?

A blind man was offered a miraculous cure by a very competent doctor.

Once the operation is over, you will be able to see, said the doctor. Then you can throw away your stick!

I don't understand you doctor, said the blind man.

I agree that I will be able to see after the operation but how will I be able to walk without my stick?

Until you begin to see, how will you know that you have no more need for the stick? Until we lose our fear of looking inward, how will we discover how tremendously powerful we really are?

Meditation is nothing but this process of looking inward. It is the process of tapping into the boundless energy and wisdom of the cosmos.

This is not a vague philosophical statement! Every biologist will agree that biochemical systems which include trees, animals, the sun and you, are communicating with their environment all the time. An invisible web of communion links all life into one vast, self-maintaining system. The intelligence that makes this happen is not something borrowed from the outside. Just as it exists in us, intelligence exists in the plants and in the molecules.

This is the mystery of life.

We live in intelligence, surrounded by intelligence. We are intelligence. We are nothing but an expression of the cosmic intelligence. If we knew how deeply we are connected to the wisdom of the cosmos, we would feel no more fear.

Like the fish searching for the ocean, we search for God outside of ourselves. We forget that we are not only the fish, but also the ocean, the water, the saltiness, and the life!

AH, NOW I SEE!

ENHANCING YOUR AWARENESS

AH, NOW I SEE!
ENHANCING YOUR AWARENESS

A few months back, a man brought his fourteen-year-old son to me. The boy had been expelled from school for hurting another child badly with a piece of glass.

When I asked the child why he did it, he gave me an answer I never expected:

He said, I was bored.

Can you imagine!

At fourteen, the child was so bored with everything that normal life had to offer, that the only thing left to explore was violence!

Extreme boredom is a special disease of our time! By the time a child is five, he or she has already learnt the meaning of the word boredom.

What does it say about them? That they have already finished seeing and doing everything of interest by the time they are five!

Along with depression, hurry and stress, boredom is a gift of our modern lifestyle. It is a typical symptom shown by the urban rich and the highly intellectual.

I asked the boy, How did you manage it? How did you manage to get bored?

To be bored requires a tremendous capacity to ignore life. Boredom is the anesthetic that numbs you to life!

Life is pulsing with life! - if only you open your eyes and see.

Have you noticed how, in moments of great personal danger, the clock seems to slow down? Suppose you have a fall or a motor accident, when you think back, every moment of that event seems to have happened in slow-motion! That's because only at that time have you called up all your faculties of awareness! Only at that time are you 100% mindful, totally aware of the moment. Only in that moment have you really lived. When you are totally open, you will find that each moment, there is something new, fresh, interesting happening. In our normal routine, days pass into weeks and weeks into months without our even noticing. But when you go on a weekend vacation, the two days seem to stretch into eternity! When you live each moment fully, you can extract the whole juice of life. Now we are just throwing away the juice, we don't know how to enjoy every moment, every drop.

The truth is, we have forgotten how to look at life as it is. We see everything around us through the coloured glasses of our own desires, habits and fears. Today, Quantum Physics goes so far as to say that reality itself is only a construct of our minds. This is what our ancient enlightened masters called maya, illusion. Maya is nothing but the distortion of reality by our own greed and fear.

In our time, we have one more joy-killer: cerebral knowledge. Our lives have become altogether too cerebral. We live too much by intellect, and too little by experience. If you notice, it is the most intellectual people who are the most easily bored. You can say, they have become blind with knowledge, because knowledge makes a theory out of everything. Knowledge tends to fit life into a box of the known and the expected. In other words, we see only what we expect to see. No wonder we find life so boring!

I am not condemning knowledge. Knowledge is essential for carrying on our daily living. It is also not wrong to feel bored. Feeing bored sometimes is normal! Like I said, boredom is a sign of the superior mind. Have you ever seen a bored buffalo? So don't feel guilty about getting bored!

What I am saying to you is, don't substitute knowledge for awareness, for experiential understanding. Don't let your intellectual approach blind you to the daily wonders of life.

To live in awareness every moment doesn't require you to be doing something very different. You don't have to have an accident or take an exotic vacation to truly experience life!

Be very clear: there is no utterly different place to go; there are no tremendously different things to do. It is how you choose to see it! So don't ask me, My life is so normal, so boring. What is there to be noticed with wonder?

You will be surprised. Perfect awareness even in your daily living can show you the wonders of life.

A small story:

> A wise man met an old lady on the village road. The lady was coming back to her home after grazing her goats. On her head, she was balancing a pot of water from the river. The wise man thought he would give her some advice.
> Why do you still busy yourself with these worldly tasks? he asked her. At your age, you should be leaving aside everything else and turning all your attention upon God!
> Who said my attention is not upon God? the lady asked. Even at this moment, when I am talking to you and herding my goats, my awareness is upon the pot I am balancing on my head, and at the same time upon God!

Bring awareness into your daily living - and each day will actually begin to look like a miracle.

Boredom is not a sign of low energy. It is a symptom of the poor utilization of the energy and abilities that you have. Existence has gifted us with boundless energy but we don't know how to use it. We don't channel it into awareness, into creativity, into productivity, into love.

It is a sin not to channel your energy in the proper direction!

You have so much energy circulating inside you; what will happen to it? If you don't utilize it, you will fall directly into *tamas* (lethargy). Then follows depression and boredom, which prompts children to hurt each other 'just to have some fun'.

It is not just children who tire of their toys in no time. We too are forever bored, forever looking for something new that can capture our interest. That's why any new product introduced in the market is sure to find takers. The success of a product is directly proportional to the number of bored people in its target market! We play not only with things; we also play with people. Almost everybody has a standard complaint that their family and friends are the most boring people in the world! We have to keep switching to new people all the time - new friends, a new neighbourhood, a new club, a new boyfriend. These days, people feel the need to change their car and their girlfriend at least once every three months! We get bored of our surroundings, bored of one another, and ultimately, we get bored of ourselves. The truth is, we find ourselves so boring that we can't spend five minutes alone. We are afraid to see how utterly uninteresting we are. All our socializing is nothing but an escape from ourselves.

Be very clear: life is not boring, only the mind is boring! It is the mind that reflects the world, and if there is dust on the mirror, how can the world appear fresh? The mind makes you insensitive to life. It is the nature of the mind to get accustomed to anything. And when you get used to something, you start taking it for granted. That's why the flowers in your own garden are never worth a second look. Your wife is never as interesting as the women you meet outside.

Today, try something new: take a walk in your garden, or on your own street. See how many things you have missed noticing till now.
How many plants are in bloom? Which colours?
How many houses are freshly painted?
What are the sounds you hear?
As you walk, be aware of every step you take.
Be aware of the sun on your face, of the breeze on your skin.
Walk with total mindfulness.
You will be amazed to see how much you have been missing all these days! Life is such a precious gift, but you have been taking it for granted. When life itself is so new and changing, how can you possibly be bored?
Mindfulness is a great meditation technique.

When you live in awareness, you don't give your mind a chance to start talking! When you enter totally into the present, the mind can't impose the past or future on you. No memories, no plans. Just total awareness of the present moment. Simply with awareness, you can fall into the experience of no-mind. With mindfulness, you can attain enlightenment!

> Somebody once asked the Buddha, We have heard so much about your powers! Are you a god?
> No, answered the Buddha.
> An avatar (incarnation of god), then?
> No, answered the Buddha.
> Then a wizard, a magician?
> No, answered the Buddha.
> Then what are you?
> I am Awake, answered the Buddha.

To be Awake is to be free. Free from ignorance, from misery, from boredom.
Preserve your sense of wonder. It is precious!
With awareness, you can see your life for the daily miracle that it is.
Simply with awareness, you can transform your world.

ASTROLOGY

AND BEYOND

DOES ASTROLOGY
HAVE A SCIENTIFIC BASIS?

ASTROLOGY AND BEYOND

DOES ASTROLOGY
HAVE A SCIENTIFIC BASIS?

Astrology is a tricky subject to handle, because there are an equal number of believers and non-believers!

To the non-believers, it has to be shown that astrology is a proven science.

The believers must be convinced that it is not the ultimate science - there is a way beyond the predictions of astrology!

I will try to do both.

Astrology has been practiced since ancient times by cultures across the world - by the Babylonians, the Greeks, the Romans, the Arabs and the Indians.

The fundamental theory of astrology is that cosmic phenomena affect life and events on Earth.

This is definitely true.

Earth is not an isolated planet. Whether we realize it or not, we are all space travelers! Events in outer space can certainly affect our lives.

How?

The sun, the moon and the planets - all have their own magnetic fields, gravitational forces and radiations, which influence the rhythms of life on Earth.

We all know that the sun and moon affect us on a daily basis. Every day, depending on the position of the sun, we experience physiological changes in temperature, heart rate, and so on.

In all cultures across the world, we find evidence of 'madness' increasing at the time of full moon. In fact, the word lunatic comes from lunar (from moon).

Experiments have proved that this is not just an empty belief. The American Institute of Medical Climatology has extensive statistical evidence that psychotic behaviour like destructive driving, arson and homicide - all increase on full moon days. Experimenters in Germany have proved that lunar phases correlate with respiratory and blood diseases, and even influence the time of death!

We have also seen that during solar flares or other disturbances on the sun, admissions to psychiatric hospitals increase sharply.

When the sun and moon can affect our physical, emotional and mental state so strongly, how can we doubt whether the planets can do the same?

In terms of chemical composition, man is made of the same material as the planets. Naturally, we respond to the changes produced in the Earth's magnetic field by other planets.

When these responses are on a day-to-day basis, they are easy to understand. But the planets can also have a long-term influence on us. This is the basis of astrological predictions.

Astrological predictions are very popular in the East, and in India almost every Hindu will have a chart of personal astrological predictions - called his horoscope. This chart is prepared when the baby is born, and predicts which are his lucky and unlucky periods, which profession he will take up, when he will get married, and so on.

Even people who agree that the planets can influence us, don't believe that we can predict these influences in advance. How can the positions of the planets during your birth determine which profession you are going to take up?

But experiments have proved it!

An experimenter called Michael Gauquelin, working in the Psychophysiological Laboratory at Strasbourg, tested 1084 famous physicians, and found that an amazing number of them were born when the planets Mars or Saturn were rising. The results were 10 million times the number expected by chance (probability theory) alone!

In another experiment, an American psychologist called Vernon Clark collected horoscopes from a large group of people in different professions.

He passed on these horoscopes to 20 astrologers for their predictions on what the person's profession might be. 17 out of 20 predicted the right profession with an accuracy that was 100 times more than that expected by chance! Clark repeated these tests, making them tougher every time. He still got the same impressive results!

In India, from ancient times, jyotisha (astrology) was used precisely for this: to determine which path a person was going to follow in life. When a child entered the gurukul (school), jyotisha was used to diagnose what kind of personality, what kind of attitude and natural aptitudes he possessed. Accordingly, he would be trained in scripture study, martial arts, business skills, or whatever suited him best. This was one reason why astrology became widespread in India.

How is this kind of prediction possible?

Just like lunar activity determines our moods to some extent, the moon and planets also exert an influence on the unborn child. Radiation of a certain wavelength can stimulate a certain area of the brain, which ultimately decides whether the person might be good at mathematics, whether he might be artistically inclined and so on. So if we know which planets were active during the period of the child's development, we can predict his future with some accuracy. This is a very basic explanation, for your understanding.

Moreover, all matter is composed of the same fundamental particles. And these particles behave in same way everywhere - whether they are part of a planet, a tree, or you! As Quantum Mechanics has proved, matter also has a kind of wave motion. So each of the planets has a unique wave motion. When two waves of different wavelengths (from different planets) meet each other and get superimposed, there will be some 'high points' (during which both waves are in harmony and their qualities are enhanced), and some 'low points' (during which they cancel out each other's influences). This is how the combined influence of various planets is calculated.

Because the waves have a regular frequency, the periods of harmony and disruption also happen at regular intervals. Using this as a basis, astrologers can predict the ups and downs of your life.

The basis of astrology is not magic, it is mathematics.

Astrology is like an equation in which the positions of the sun, the moon and the planets can be seen as variables. By making complex calculations based on these positions and their influences, a competent astrologer can definitely get verifiable results.

Like any other information, astrological data can be statistically analysed and quantified.

But the major problem is that data from an enormous number of variables have to be combined, weighed and worked out in various permutations. The individual and combined influence of planets have to be considered. Moreover, the planets not only influence us, but also each other.

This is a very difficult task, so most astrologers these days just use a few basic variables, which ultimately give inaccurate results. Above all, the results are open to interpretation, which makes the whole science less reliable. These are the reasons that astrology is not seen as a credible science today.

I am not here to prove or disprove astrology.

I am here to demystify it.

Astrology can give a fair idea of the influences working on you. It can show you the problem, but it can't show you the solution.

Meditation can show you the solution.

Meditation is nothing but a way of connecting to the cosmic energy, the force that guides the sun, the planets and you.

When you function in harmony with the cosmic energy, you will naturally have better protection from these influences. Anyone who goes out in the rain is likely to catch a cold but the person who does not resist the rain as harmful, can simply remain unaffected by it.

Does everybody go mad at full moon?

Of course not! The full moon affects only the already imbalanced mind. If your condition is stable, these factors simply don't affect you.

Meditation strengthens you not only spiritually, but physically, mentally and emotionally as well.

With meditation, you can go beyond astrology.

DON'T DO YOUR DUTY!
DUTY VS. RESPONSIBILITY

DON'T DO YOUR DUTY!
DUTY VS. RESPONSIBILITY

There's an old Indian tale:

A king was on a hunting trip in a forest, when all of a sudden he was enchanted by the lovely notes of a flute. Trying to trace the source of the music, he came upon a man sitting alone outside his hut, playing his music for the river and the wind.

The king asked the man, You play the flute wonderfully! Who taught you to play?

Oh, no one! smiled the man. When I sit here and watch this beauty, the song arises on its own. This is just my way of expressing my joy!

The king was impressed. No musician in his palace could play so beautifully. He decided that it might be a good idea to take the man back to the palace with him.

In spite of the man's protests, the king took him back to the palace. His sole duty was to entertain the king with his delightful music. The king arranged for the man to have one of the finest rooms in the palace, overlooking the royal gardens.

The next morning, the king woke early and summoned the man to the garden.

Come on, play me a song! he ordered.

Obediently, the man struggled with the flute - but no music would emerge from it!

The king was astonished.

What is the matter? Is the royal garden lacking in beauty? Do you have no inspiration to play? he demanded.

No, Your Majesty. The garden is beautiful, but my music can no longer match its beauty, said the man unhappily.

Why? asked the king.

Because yesterday my music was a joy, today it has become my duty!

DUTY is truly an ugly word!

No other word has such a tremendous capacity to transform joy into misery.

Duty must be the most abused word of our time.

In the history of civilization, so much has been spoken and written about the importance of doing one's duty that it is time to ask: what actually is Duty?

Duty is nothing but doing the right thing for the wrong reason!

Duty arises when a sense of values is imposed upon us from the outside. When you find yourself doing the 'correct' thing, but with no sense of joy or fulfillment, it usually means that you are just fulfilling a duty. And without exception, every person secretly rebels against the concept of having to perform one's duty.

But duty is a double-edged sword!

When you do something merely out of a sense of duty, you usually end up feeling resentful and frustrated. But if you don't do it, you feel guilty! Both ways, duty doesn't give you a chance at happiness.

How do we find ourselves trapped in the snare of duty?

The sad truth is, most of us don't have the courage to live life on our own terms. We seek refuge in so many institutions - social, moral, legal. But we forget that nothing in life comes for free! In return, these institutions impose 'duties' upon us. Ultimately, our controls are always in someone else's hands! But we live in such deep unconsciousness that we don't even realize we are trapped.

A man once approached the Buddha, seeking sannyas. He

wanted to become the Buddha's disciple.

The Buddha smiled and told him, Alright, I will accept you. But on one condition. First, I want you to go and kill your family and friends, and come back to me.

The man was astonished. What did the Buddha mean by that? Was the Buddha asking the man to go and physically kill his family and friends?

NO! What he meant was, Go and kill the voices of society which are inside you, continuously instructing and disturbing you. Kill them psychologically, not actually. Remove their influence from your Being.

Take a close look at your life.

How many people are sitting inside your head, giving you instructions on how to live and what to do? How many people are telling you what is right and wrong for you? Who are the people controlling your life?

Your parents, your children, your spouse, your friends, strangers, society, law. All the writers of all the moral books you have read, all the speakers of all the discourses you have listened to are sitting there!

There will be enough people to tell you what to sacrifice, and for whom: for your family, your children, for society, for your motherland, for an ideology, for God...!

Every patriot thinks it his duty to kill! Even Hitler considered it his sacred duty to kill all the Jews on the planet.

At least in war, people kill their enemies for the sake of duty. You are killing yourself!

Ask yourself this question consciously: what are my real reasons for doing my duty?

The desire to please someone?

The fear of disapproval?

A sense of guilt?

Pride in being morally superior?

Make a list of all the duties you have been doing for the past five years.

Mark the ones you are doing NOW.

Ask yourself: has it been worth it? Have they helped you feel more joyous, more fulfilled? Or have they left you with a vague sense of resentment?

Now, do this. This is important.

Make a note of all the times when doing something for someone else has brought you tremendous joy.

Which are those times? Who are those people?

You will find that those were always the times when you performed an action most selflessly, when you voluntarily shifted the focus of your attention from yourself to the other. It might be anyone - your beloved, your child, your best friend.

Without exception, when an action is performed out of love, there is never a feeling of resentment. There is never the burden of duty. Love is the key that can free you from the prison of duty!

This is not a moral statement.

Whether you believe it or not, whether you accept it or not, we are all deeply interconnected.

Just as every organism in the Earth's ecosystem is interconnected on the physical plane, we are intimately connected to each other without our awareness.

This is the reality of our existence.

To recognise this is a sign of maturity.

When you experience love for another, you make this leap into awareness naturally!

When people talk to me about duty, I tell them,

What you are doing is the right thing.

But the reason you are doing it for is wrong!

Live out of Consciousness, not out of Conscience.

Don't trust your fear. Trust your intelligence.

Even without fear or guilt, you will automatically stay on the correct path.

You may ask me, but most of my duties involve people I love! Then why do I find it such a strain?

Because, somewhere along the way, in the push and pull of daily living, you have lost focus of your love!

You have replaced your natural sense of responsibility with an enforced sense of duty.

There is a tremendous difference between responsibility and duty.

Responsibility is literally the ability to respond. It is your capacity to respond spontaneously to the needs of another.

Responsibility is what inspires a man to rush into a burning house to rescue a stranger. No sense of duty could have accomplished that!

Responsibility is a natural offshoot of love. It arises when you recognize that you are not separate from the other.

It springs from the deep understanding:

You are, therefore I am.

Once the sense of responsibility arises, the word duty will vanish on its own.

EVERY BODY KNOWS...!
TRUST YOUR BODY'S INTELLIGENCE

EVERY BODY KNOWS...!
TRUST YOUR BODY'S INTELLIGENCE

A while back I saw an advertisement for a popular sports gear brand. The picture showed a man preparing hard for a competitive event. The headline said:

If your body asks you to stop, tell your body to shut up.

How often do you ask your body to shut up?

Most of the time! Is it not?

From the moment you wake up in the morning, it is a tug-of-war with your body.

Do you realise, man is the only creature who needs an alarm clock to wake up in the morning - because he is so completely out of tune with nature's rhythm!

When you get up, your body is screaming for more sleep. It hasn't had the time to recover after that late night you had. But it's Monday morning, so you tell your body to shut up.

After spending hours staring at the computer in office, your eyes feel dry and tired. But you have a project report to be finished. So what do you tell your body? Yes, Shut up!

When you overeat or drink too much at a party, when you sit up late watching television, when you push yourself to work even on a day when you don't feel well - you are continuously ignoring the warnings of the body.

These days we all take pride in telling our bodies to shut up. We tax our lungs with polluted air, our stomachs with spicy and unhealthy food, our livers with alcohol. To some extent, our bodies learn to cope with the assault by becoming less and less sensitive. That's why our tolerance threshold is climbing every day. We need larger quantities of alcohol to get drunk, and higher doses of painkillers to stop feeling pain. If we knew how deeply our body and mind influence each other, we would treat our body better!

Our body has tremendous intelligence, gathered over 600 million years of evolution.

The processes we usually call 'conscious processes' are the ones controlled by our central nervous system - the brain and the spinal cord. This includes voluntary actions, thinking, and so on.

But conscious processes are a small minority of the action that is going on in our body! The vast majority of the processes are 'unconscious', and are mostly controlled by the autonomous nervous system. These processes, like breathing, digesting food, keeping our balance when we walk, all run beautifully without our control or even our awareness. Imagine, if we had to worry about running our bodies, we would never get anything else done!

How do you think all this happens?

This is the miracle of body intelligence.

Just watch your body!

Every single cell in your body is gifted with the intelligence to carry on its own unique functions. When an infection attacks the body, your white blood cells swing into action on their own, long before you are even aware of the danger.

But the sad truth is, we have lost trust in our own body wisdom!

The day you have a cold, or feel a headache coming up, you automatically pop a pill. Why? Don't you see, your body is carrying on the work of a huge industrial plant! It is an ecosystem in itself. When your body can digest food, pump blood and fight infections on a regular basis, can't it heal a simple headache on its own?

If you enter the amazingly complex world of DNA, you will see that your emotions, your memories, even your opinions are strongly controlled by your body! DNA are the carriers of our genetic code. They carry imprints not only of physical characteristics, but also of mental states. Geneticists say that every person has a unique perception of the world that is built up by his DNA!

Not only does the body influence the mind, the mind also exerts tremendous influence on the body.

A person who has been cured of a disease, or rehabilitated after a drug addiction, still carries some memories of the disease in his body. In the same way, if you worry constantly, the negativity triggered by the worries can solidify in your body and being. This is what we call depression. That's why depressed people often can't tell why they are depressed. Long after the problem has been solved, the stress associated with it remains in their memory as an energy blockage, both physical and mental.

Not just depression, but practically every disease is equally influenced by both body and mind. In fact, over 85% of our diseases are psychosomatic in nature. Not just headaches or heart disease, but peptic ulcers, skin and respiratory allergies, even cancer is influenced by our thinking.

The mind has unimaginable power to cause or cure physical ailments!

An experiment was performed in Japan on a group of people who were allergic to a certain plant. The participants were blindfolded and leaves from different plants were placed upon their skin. Each time, the researchers told the participants which leaf they were placing on them.

Amazingly, they found that in most cases the allergy was caused by the mention of the name of the plant, rather than by the actual plant. When they placed the allergy-causing leaf on the skin, but told the patient it was a harmless leaf, the subject did not develop the allergy. On the other hand, even if a harmless leaf was placed on the skin, and the subject was told that it was the allergy-causing leaf, he would instantly break out in a rash!

In another amazing experiment with a boy having multiple personalities, psychologist Daniel Goleman found that the boy's allergies could be switched on and off depending on which personality was dominant at that time! The same mind would give the body orders to act allergic or non-allergic, depending on which reaction suited that particular personality.

Modern medical science uses techniques like the PET scan to track chemical changes in your brain under different circumstances. Researchers have found that each time you recall a different memory, or experience a strong emotion, it triggers a different chemical pattern in your brain.

Not just that, the news spreads throughout your body immediately. Whether you are feeling happy, angry or sad, a signal is sent out instantly to every cell in your body. So your body is actually a changing reflection of what you are thinking at that moment!

Just like psychosomatic diseases show us how our unconscious mind controls our conscious functions, meditation teaches us how to use the conscious mind to control 'unconscious' functions. In yoga and Zen, there are techniques by which you can consciously control your pulse rate, digestion, metabolism, body temperature and even your degree of sensitivity to pain!

Actually, there is nothing miraculous about these phenomena. They appear miraculous to us only because we are unaware of the deep relationship that exists between our body and mind.

Both body and mind are only expressions of the same Consciousness. They cannot, and do not function separately. Unless we respect both equally, we can never be complete, integrated individuals.

In modern civilization, we are developing our minds at the expense of our bodies. Anthropologists say that a few hundred generations from now, we may be reduced to creatures with giant brains and stunted bodies, because the brain is the only part of the body we are using!

Abusing the body is not a modern problem. The body has traditionally been condemned as the grossest part of ourselves. We always blame the body for disturbing us, pulling us into *maya*, towards the temptations of the world. Right from ancient times, yogis felt it was necessary to neglect the body to attain to spirituality. So they would torture the body, deprive the body, and keep repeating to themselves, I am not the body, I am not the body. This is one path, but it works for very few.

I say, the way to spirituality is only through the body!

The body is the boat that is going to carry you across the river of *samsara*, of Life. If your boat itself is leaking and faulty, how will you ever cross the river? Unless you learn to respect your body, how can you go beyond the body?

Enter into a deep, loving relationship with your body.

Sri Ramakrishna says beautifully:

There are two ways to cross the river of maya.

One is by summoning all your strength and leaping across. The other way is to stand before it with folded palms and request, O Maya, please allow me to get across!

This is the path of respect and tolerance.

Make peace with your body.

Drop the idea of controlling your body.

Trust in your body wisdom.

Only by deeply understanding your body, with clarity and compassion, will you find a way to go beyond it.

GET UP AND DANCE!

BE SPONTANEOUS

GET UP AND DANCE!

BE SPONTANEOUS

The famous Zen master Bankei, wandering in Japan, arrives in a
new town.

(My stories are most often drawn from Zen, because no other
religion has taken to life so beautifully, has met life with such
reverence and courage and humour.

Zen is a love affair with life!)

When people hear that the Zen master is in their town, they
come to see him, and say,

Beloved master, we have heard so much about you! We hear that
simply by being in your presence, people feel immensely joyful.
They get healed of diseases miraculously. They feel their wishes
are coming true! What is the special meditation you practice to
attain these powers?

The master replies simply, When I'm hungry, I eat. When I'm
sleepy, I sleep. That is my meditation.

Zen masters usually talk like this! And just as you are confused right
now, the people who hear him are also confused. What could possibly
be easier than eating and sleeping? All their lives, they have been eating
and sleeping! And here was this great master, calling it a powerful
meditation technique!

So they beg for an explanation.

And the master asks them, Do you really eat when you're hungry? Do
you sleep when you're sleepy?

Do we?

When do we usually eat?

When lunch is ready; when we have the time; when the clock says so. Without even realizing it, we live our life within a set behavioural pattern. Even for such personal acts as eating and sleeping, we depend on a schedule that we've built up for ourselves! This pattern that controls our life is nothing but what we call habits.

There are so many people who simply can't start their day without a cup of tea or coffee! If they can't get their tea first thing in the morning, they develop a headache, they can't get through the day. All of us have our pet habits. We call them 'our habits', and think that we are in charge of them, but actually they are the ones in charge of us!

Carried to an insane extreme, an obsession with habit can ruin our lives. In psychiatry, this is known as Obsessive Compulsive Disorder (OCD). People who suffer from this disorder tend to continuously repeat the same act. It might be a simple act like washing their hands, or checking to see if a door has been properly locked, but they will do it again and again as if their life depended on it. Autistic people can become gravely disturbed if anything in their environment is even slightly changed; even if the furniture has been rearranged in a room, it is enough to set them off.

Don't laugh off this behaviour as madness!

Be very clear: between the so-called normal and disturbed people, it is only a difference of degree and a small one, at that!

Habits numb you to the changing reality of life. To act out of habit is to miss out on all the opportunities for change that life creates for us every moment.

Even at the most challenging moments of our life, we tend to function out of habit!

A small story:

> A pickpocket died and went to Heaven. St. Peter, guarding the pearly gates, stopped him. He reminded the man that he'd been cheating people all his life, and deserved to go to Hell instead. But the pickpocket begged forgiveness and promised to transform himself into a new person. At last St. Peter took pity on him. Alright, he told the man wearily, Go on in. But first, would you mind returning my purse?

***

In our 'civilized' society, we place a ridiculous value on consistency. Usually, people are so proud of being consistent! They boast about having woken up at the same time for the past 30 years; they boast about how they have been communists or atheists or whatever, since their school days.

Consistent people are the most boring people! When someone is always consistent, it can mean only one of two things:

(a) He was born perfect, and doesn't need to change a single thing about himself throughout his life, or (b) He is clinging to his old ideas, out of pride or fear.

I don't think that anyone can claim to be already perfect? So the only other reason would be, the fear of change.

Habits represent the familiar, the accepted patterns of life. Habits symbolize security. That's why we cling to our habits for dear life!

It requires great courage to live without habits, without beliefs. It means that you don't need an idea to tell you what is right, or what to do. But we are so afraid of making mistakes, that we destroy our spontaneity.

I ask you, even a baby is not afraid of taking new steps, so why are you?

The joy of living is to open yourself to the ebb and flow of life. Life is insecurity! Learn to enjoy the insecurity of life, and you will never feel fear.

As we grow older, we tend to resist change more and more. We feel threatened by change, because it goes against our solid ideas of right and wrong, or what works and what doesn't work for us.

We forget that Life is essentially non-paradoxical. We find it paradoxical only when we compare today to what we learnt yesterday, or to what we plan for tomorrow. It is only when we try to confine a situation to our own expectations that we see contradictions.

A small story:

> In a village, there lived two sadhus (holy men). One of them was very proud of his knowledge of the scriptures and logic. He was forever spouting philosophy. The other was a simple, happy man who mingled with the villagers and lived a life of peace.
> One day, the two met on the road leading to the market.
> Where are you headed? asked the first sadhu, hoping to start a philosophical debate.
> Where my feet lead me! replied the other joyfully.
> The first sadhu was stumped. What did he mean by that? Was he presenting him with a philosophical riddle? How to answer him?
> He went home and spent the whole day pondering the meaning of the sadhu's statement. With great trouble, he crafted an equally intelligent counter-statement.
> The next day, he triumphantly approached the other sadhu on the same road.
> Where are you headed? he repeated.
> Where the wind takes me! replied the other sweetly.
> This was too much! The first sadhu was dismayed. He had such a perfectly planned counter-argument, and now the other had changed his statement! So he went back home and prepared himself to face this new challenge.
> The third day, he waylaid the other sadhu and repeated the question,
> Where are you headed?
> Oh, just to the market, to get some vegetables!, replied the other sadhu, laughing.

Such is life!

In life, the answers change everyday. When change is the only reality of life, how can you plan ahead?

In Chinese Taoism, life is symbolically represented by the yin-yang. Yin and yang represent the opposing principles of life - negative and positive, darkness and light, contraction and expansion. But the beautiful thing about the yin-yang is that the two aspects are continuously flowing into each other, changing every moment. There's always a little yin in yang, and vice-versa; just like life, which is always fluid, always changing.

In an experiment conducted by a behavioral psychologist, two groups of people were asked to listen to the same piece of music and respond in whatever way they felt like - by dancing, singing along, laughing, waving their arms about or just sitting. The only difference was, in the second group, all the people were blindfolded.

Needless to say, less than a fifth of the participants in the first group responded to the music in a truly spontaneous manner, while almost everybody in the second group let themselves go.

We have grown so afraid of looking foolish or out of place, of going against the current, that we have simply lost the capacity to respond to the moment without fear or prejudice.

The funny thing is, these days a lot of people are waking up to the importance of being spontaneous but by now we have forgotten how to 'do it'!

Everywhere you find teenagers wearing T-shirts saying Do your own thing, but in truth they are terrified of not doing the accepted thing, of not fitting in.

I tell you, you don't have to learn to be spontaneous! We were all born with an innate ability to enjoy life, moment to moment. Somewhere along the way, between personal habits and the rules of society, we lost that ability. And every generation does this to the next.

We have a great capacity for destroying the spontaneity of our children.

Don't sing now, papa is sleeping!
Who asked you to draw on the wall?
Go to bed RIGHT NOW!
Is this the time to be playing outdoors?

We have no idea what a dangerous thing we are doing to them!
Be very clear: to be spontaneous is not to live lawlessly.
It is not the liberty to disrupt the basic laws of social living.
Spontaneity is not anarchy, or self-indulgence.
To be spontaneous is simply to drop your habits.
Drop your prejudices.
Drop your yesterday and your tomorrow.
See today with a clear eye, with an unburdened mind.
Respond to the rich unfolding of life, moment to moment.
Embrace change - and life will embrace you!

KEEP QUIET AND LISTEN
LEARNING TO LISTEN BETTER

KEEP QUIET AND LISTEN
LEARNING TO LISTEN BETTER

Take a good look at your life.
How many hours a day do you spend talking?
And how many hours do you spend listening?

Most of the day, we are either talking or trying to talk!
Have you noticed, whenever people are in a group, every person feels an intense need to monopolize the conversation.
Talking is a way of controlling the environment. Most people use talking as a way of showing their power. Not just by what they say, but how they say it, how long they talk - and how much they can control others' talking! No wonder, 'Shut up' is seen as the most humiliating term of abuse! If you are not allowed to talk, you feel as if you have been deprived of something very important, because everybody is competing to vomit his ideas and opinions on everyone else! We have all built up a whole storehouse of borrowed opinions from books and media but rarely do we get someone who is willing to listen to them!

When you eat, but cannot digest the food what happens?
You have to vomit it out!
In the same way, if you have read someone else's philosophies and ideas, but they have not become your personal experience, you haven't digested them, you end up vomiting them out.
Talking is not just to other people. When you are not talking to someone else, you are talking to yourself and that's even more dangerous. Talking

to ourselves is what we all do, practically every minute of our waking time. All our plans and worries are nothing but - talking to ourselves! Talking to yourself is nothing but the inner chatter, the flow of thoughts that keeps playing in your mind, continuously disturbing you. At least with outer conversations, there is a break sometimes. But this inner chatter is continuous. It can drive you mad! Actually, many times, speaking to others is just a way of escaping from your own being, from your own inner chatter. That is why so much talking is going on in the world!

Today, there is an acute shortage of listening in the world!

More than a century ago, Bertrand Russel predicted that listening will become the highest paid profession of our time. And it has happened! Today, practically every person especially in the West has a personal listener. People pay huge sums to the 'shrink' or counselor, not for solving their problems but simply for listening to them. Because who else is there to listen? Today, no one has the time to listen, to give attention to the other.

Your attention is your energy!

When you are so low on energy that you don't even have enough for yourself, how are you going to give energy to others?

Most of the time, you don't even hear when others are talking to you! All the time, there is so much being spoken around you if only you can listen!

Talking is not always through words.

In fact, the most important part of our communication with one another is nonverbal.

When your wife brings you coffee in the morning, listen to her.

Not just to her words, even to her actions.

Does she put the cup down with a bang? What is she trying to tell you?

Is your child throwing a loud tantrum every time you have guests? Don't listen to his tantrum; listen to him. He's trying to tell you that he needs more of your time, your attention. Tantrums are the only way he can get attention right now. Is there something you can do about it?

There is a famous Zen koan (riddle) which says:
If a tree falls in a forest and there is no one to hear it, does it make a noise?

Recently a harassed young mother who attended one of my programs came and asked me jokingly: Swamiji, if a child falls in a forest and there is no one to hear him, does he make a noise?!
We are also no different from children! All our noise, all our talking is nothing but a way of asking for attention. If everybody learns to listen, there will be no need to talk!
Never mind listening to others - are you listening to yourself? For instance, do you listen to your own body anymore? When you go to a party and overeat or drink too much, you can hear your body screaming at you to stop. When you sit up late watching television, your body is crying, Enough, I need rest! In fact, all diseases are nothing but your body's way of asking for your attention, for your concern.
But do you listen?
When you get home from work, you hear yourself slamming the door hard. Do you do the same when you get home after a movie? That slamming noise speaks volumes about how you feel about your job. How can you change that?
And unless you listen, how will you even know that something is wrong?
We have forgotten the gentle art of listening.

Listening is not just about listening to someone else or yourself talk.
Listening is also about listening to the silence that is in us, around us.
All our talking is just waves upon an ocean of beautiful silence. Have you ever heard that silence?
Create space and time in your life for listening to silence.
Make a practice of spending some time everyday doing this.
Welcome natural sounds into your silence.
Don't listen for the sake of hearing anything, for the sake of getting some information.

Just be aware; be open to the silence.
It is in silence that you learn the most. Only in silence can you truly understand life, poetry, nature.
The Zen master Basho says in a haiku:
Sitting silent, doing nothing, and the grass grows by itself.
This silence is not a passive silence. It is a positive, listening silence. It is the silence of deep communion.
There is a big difference between communication and communion. Communication is what we are getting better and better at these days! Communication is the science of conveying information in words and actions. Communion is the pure transfer of energy it is beyond words. Nowadays we have mastered complex communication through telephones, mobile networks, internet but we don't know the simple ways of being in communion with each other!
Communion is the gift of the master.
It does not need words.
In fact, the master can give you more with his spells of silence than with his words if you know how to listen.
When you listen to the master, listen as you would listen to the birds or the wind. When you listen to the birds, do you believe or disbelieve? Do you agree or disagree? Neither! You simply allow. It is not an intellectual process. Simply listen with openness, with receptivity and you will automatically enter into deep communion with the master.

There is a verse in the Dakshinamurti Stotram about the communion between a young master and his disciples:
Chitram vadataror mooley
Vriddhah shishyaa gurur yuvah
Gurostu maunam vyaakhyaanam
Shishyaastu chinnah samshayah
(Beneath the banyan tree they sit
the disciples old men, the guru a mere youth!
The guru speaks through Silence alone
But lo! The disciples' questions dissolve on their own!)

This is true communion.
When your listening is total, there is no longer any need for words.
Where there is communion, words drop away naturally.

When the great Buddhist master Bodhidharma was on his deathbed, he called four of his disciples to find out who had listened best, who had learnt the most from the master.

He put a common question to them: What is truth?

The first disciple said, Truth is that which is beyond affirmation and negation.

You have my skin, said the master to the disciple.

The second disciple said, Truth is that which once seen, is forever seen.

You have my flesh, said the master.

Truth is no-thing, said the third disciple.

You have my bones, said the master to him.

The fourth disciple said nothing.

In deep gratitude for the learning he had received, he simply bowed before the master and stood in communion with him.

After a while, the master spoke.

You have my marrow, he told the disciple.

Silence is a beautiful way of entering into meditation. In fact, silence itself is a great meditation technique. It is a great healing and rejuvenating power.

In silence, you achieve what Jesus calls the peace that passeth understanding.

As they say, sweet words are silver, but silence is golden.

So the next time you open your mouth to talk, first ask yourself whether it improves upon the silence!

LAUGH YOUR WAY
TO GOD!
THE INCREDIBLE
POWER OF LAUGHTER

LAUGH YOUR WAY TO GOD!
THE INCREDIBLE POWER OF LAUGHTER

When was the last time you had a really good laugh?
A big, rumbling laugh that rose right up from your belly, and left you shaking uncontrollably with mirth?

These days, we have forgotten how to laugh.
Our laughter is only an extended smile - a social necessity. Even when we laugh, we are usually laughing at someone, or simply fulfilling a duty. Laughter has been replaced by giggles and sniggers.

> In an office, the boss tells a joke. The whole team starts roaring with laughter, except one young lady who just sits there looking bored.
> What's the matter? Why aren't you laughing? asks the boss in surprise.
> I don't have to, replies the lady casually. I'm quitting next week!

Jokes apart, laughter has tremendous potential that we have forgotten how to use.
It is an excellent way of connecting to people!
Look around you. The smartest marketing experts, the best orators, the most effective advertisements use humour to get their message across. When a leader joins his team in laughter, he easily breaks the barriers that exist between himself and them.

The truth is, even the most radical ideas, when presented in a humorous manner, are more easily accepted by people.

As the saying goes, if you want to fill an extra handful of rice in an already full rice-sack, you'll need to shake it up a bit. In much the same way, when people are already overwhelmed with heavy philosophies (like all of us are!), a little laughter can provide that 'shaking up', it can open their minds so that fresh ideas can settle more easily.

In earlier times, kings and learned men were well aware of the importance of laughter. No wonder every great king had in his court a popular court-jester - who was often the sharpest and wisest of the king's advisors. The 'royal fools' of Shakespearean plays, and our Indian jesters, Tenali Raman and Birbal, all had the art of presenting profound truths with charming and compassionate humour.

Not everyone has the wonderful capacity to laugh, and to create laughter around themselves. Most of us are afraid to laugh, especially when we are with strangers - because laughter exposes you.

Laughter exposes the innocent, vulnerable You hidden inside you.

Those who find it difficult to laugh have no idea what a gift they've lost. Believe me, there is no business more serious than the business of laughter - it is seriously important to be able to laugh!

As the joke goes, Learn to laugh at your problems. At least you'll always have something to laugh about!

People who don't mind laughing at themselves are truly blessed, because they have found a way to go beyond the ego. Laughter is no more than an overflowing of health, of abundant energy. Laughter blossoms as a natural result of being at ease with yourself and your surroundings. That's why happy, smiling people are usually the most creative and spontaneous.

I'm reminded of a street play I once watched in my childhood. In our Indian villages, street plays are almost always drawn from the ancient epics.

One of the most popular episodes from the Mahabharata is the Draupadi Vastraharana, where the villain Dushassana tries to disrobe Queen Draupadi in full view of the royal court. Having lost their wife to the villain in a treacherous game of dice, Draupadi's five husbands are forced to look on helplessly. Ultimately Draupadi appeals to Lord Krishna, and he blesses her by making her saree endless in length, so that no matter how much of it the villain unwinds, still more cloth remains to protect her modesty. Thus it is that the villains are defeated by the grace of God.

During one rendition of this enormously popular scene, it so happened that the regular Krishna was absent and a stand-in Krishna had to be roped in at the last minute.

In villages, both male and female roles are traditionally performed by men, and Draupadi was a young man who was, naturally, wearing a pair of pants beneath his fancy sarees.

When the villains swung into action, the visiting Krishna panicked and forgot to dole out the 'miraculous' additional lengths of cloth from backstage. As a result, in ten seconds flat, Queen Draupadi was standing before an astonished village audience in an embroidered blouse and a pair of well-worn pants!

But Draupadi was a seasoned actor with a great sense of humour. Even before the audience could react, he fell on his knees and cried out, Hail Krishna, Protector of the Weak! Refuge of the Wronged! You have preserved my modesty by transforming me into a man! Thank you, thank you!

Needless to say, never had the Draupadi Vastraharana scene received the thunderous applause it got that day!

* * * * *

Seriousness is truly a disease.

Have you ever seen a serious child? Children have a great ability to find something funny in every situation - especially when you have guests at home! And we adults, who can't see what is so funny, try to force them to stop laughing.

This is where the problem begins! Suppression of laughter is the beginning of disease.

Just a few weeks ago, a man approached me in my ashram with his teenaged son. His son was suffering from severe depression. At the age of fifteen, the boy had already tried to commit suicide three times. Depression is the special gift of our century! In no other time and age would you find healthy young men and women getting so tired of life that they want to kill themselves. Anyway, the boy's father had tried every possible treatment, with no results. He appealed to me to heal the boy.

I asked the father to leave the boy in the ashram with me for a few days. During that period, I spent time with the boy every day - sharing jokes! I gave him joke books to read; I asked him to go around the ashram and interact with the ashramites. Every day, we would meet and have an informal 'jokes session'. In ten days' time, the boy was completely cured of his depression. This actually happened!

Laughter has great therapeutic value. Today, the healing effects of laughter are being acknowledged by doctors and psychiatrists worldwide. The number of Laughter Clubs that have mushroomed worldwide will testify to that!

The deep, chaotic breathing induced by laughter produces positive vibrations in our body, relaxes the belly and improves digestion. Laughing also cleanses out the manipuraka chakra, the subtle energy center in our navel area, which is also the seat of worry and depression. The simple act of laughing has the power to unlock deep-rooted psychological suppressions. Laughter is a natural healing power that Nature has gifted to us.

But laughing has more than just health benefits.

Laughter is also a proven meditation technique.

In fact, in Zen monasteries, it is compulsory for all the monks to spend some time every day laughing.

A small story:

> Once there was a conference of Buddhist monks on the meaning of true spirituality. Each monk went up on stage and made long speeches, practically putting all the others to sleep. Finally, it was the turn of a particular Zen monk to speak. What do you think he did?
> He simply started laughing!
> Laughing, laughing with all his Being.
> The laughter just rose up from his belly. He started shaking uncontrollably with laughter.
> And his laughter was so infectious, soon all the others in the room started laughing, without even knowing why.
> Without their even being aware of it, the common laughter of all the monks produced a huge wave of positive energy in the room. The monks reached a state of tremendous elevation. In the course of the laughter, they experienced a moment of no-mind. The Zen monk declared, This is true spirituality.

Laughter is the highest spiritual quality. It can lead you to enlightenment! In fact, laughter is called the royal route to enlightenment. Because laughter is the easiest and most powerful way we have of connecting with the prapancha shakti, the boundless energy of all Existence.

So keep laughing always!

NOTHING COMPARES
TO YOU!
SAY NO TO JEALOUSY

NOTHING COMPARES TO YOU!
SAY NO TO JEALOUSY

Q. Swamiji, how can I stop comparing myself to others and being miserable?

At least you have realized that comparison only brings misery - that is a good beginning!

Let me answer you with a story:

> A man came to a spiritual master with a question very similar to yours.
> The wise man took him out into the garden, where a rose bush and a thorny plant were growing side by side. He told him,
> These are your teachers. They can teach you what you need to learn.
> The man was astonished.
> What do you mean, Master? he asked.
> The Master said,
> For five years, this rose-bush and this thorny plant have existed side by side. But not once have I heard the rose-bush complaining that it wanted to become a thorny plant, or the thorny plant wanting to become like the rose-bush. Each has accepted its own reality without complaint, without comparison.

Accept yourself as you are.
Only then can you be whole, you will be complete.
When you see yourself as unique and complete, the need to compare will drop automatically.

Buddha makes a statement of tremendous significance. He says: nothing exists except in relationship. Everything is relative, and draws its meaning only from its relationship with something else.

What are the words you use to compare yourself to others? Beautiful, poor, clever, unlucky, young, weak and so on.

Now, imagine yourself on some new planet, where nobody lived but you. Would you then be beautiful or ugly? Tall or short? Rich or poor? Without comparison, these words naturally lose their meaning. Because they are only concepts formulated by the mind, they have no real existence.

Try this: close your eyes for a few moments. Imagine yourself all alone in the world. Do you feel ugly or beautiful inside? Foolish or wise? Where are all these concepts then? Only the fact that you exist remains - because that is the only truth. To compare yourself with someone else is foolishness, because you can never be anyone else - and no one else can be you!

The funny thing is, we never compare ourselves to flowers or birds or mountains; so why do we compare ourselves to other people? I have yet to come across a singer who felt jealous of a koel, or a dancer who wished she were a peacock! When we can truly welcome and enjoy all else in nature that is beautiful, how come we can't enjoy the unique loveliness of each other? Why do we feel so intensely threatened by another's beauty or wealth or talent?

This is nothing but simple social conditioning. Brought up in a competitive world, we tend to imagine that the more someone else has of something, the less there is for us!

The Dalai Lama observes beautifully: most people behave as if there is a limited quantity of happiness available in the world! If someone else is happy, we feel as if our personal share of happiness is being depleted! So we go about with a long face, feeling miserable about ourselves. On the contrary, if we were to experience joy each time another person attained something, our own happiness would be multiplied millions of times by the entire population of the world!

Comparison can be of two kinds: constructive comparison and destructive comparison.

Constructive comparison is essential and desirable.

In a practical sense, it gives you a yardstick against which to measure yourself. It provides the spur, the stimulus to improve. Without comparing, how can you have a realistic appreciation of yourself?

Destructive comparison results from the inability to accept reality. In this big wide world, someone is sure to be better than you at whatever you do. 99.99% chances are that you're not the world's best mathematician, the fastest runner or the most talented painter. Does that mean that you enjoy these things any less?

To focus only on what you're lacking simply means that you're on your way to a massive inferiority complex. And who needs it?

Look around you. Do you know anyone else who is exactly the same as you? Don't you see how special you are? If you are comparing yourself to others and feeling miserable, it simply means that you aren't appreciating yourself enough!

A small story:

> One Zen master had a disciple who was intelligent, diligent and sincere. His only problem was that he had no patience with the long and arduous techniques for attaining enlightenment.
> Every day he would approach the master and ask him,
> Just tell me master, when will I become like Buddha?
> The master would simply smile and offer no answer.
> Working day and night, practising every technique according to the master's instructions, and still finding no answer, the disciple became crazed with the thirst for enlightenment.

Finally, one day he decided that the quest was simply not worth it.
He went to the master and demanded,
Tell me one thing before I leave. Am I ever going to become like
Buddha or not?
In answer, the master slapped the disciple furiously across the
face.
In that instant, the disciple awakened to his true nature!

What did the master mean by that slap?
Was he angry with the disciple for hoping for too much?
NO. The master simply had to jolt the disciple into the awareness that
he was already a Buddha! How can you want to become something you
already are?
You are so out of touch with your inner being that you have forgotten
how extraordinary you really are.
Once you realise this, the need to compare dies naturally.
Even if you wanted to compare, each person is so different - where is a
common point of reference?
So drop the attitude of comparison.
Remember, you are truly unique - just like everyone else!

NOTHING MYSTERIOUS!
TRADITION DEMYSTIFIED

NOTHING MYSTERIOUS!
TRADITION DEMYSTIFIED

NOTHING MYSTERIOUS
TRADITION DEMYSTIFIED

Q. Swamiji, do you agree with idol worship?

First of all, be very clear: what we call 'idol worship' is not the worship of idols!

It is worship *through* idols.

Obviously, no idol worshipper is worshipping the idol, the statue itself.

He is worshipping the Divine, which has been given a visible form in the idol.

Is that a foolish thing?

Let us look deeply into the matter.

As we know, all life springs from the same source. Everything in the universe is created from the same raw materials, and has a common underlying structure. You may not be aware of this, because we only see the surface variations. As a part of the universe, we are like tiny mirrors that reflect the exact composition and structure of the universe. Understand this concept clearly.

Everything in Existence is linked.

The universe is composed of five major elements, five major energies - earth, water, fire, air and ether (space). All these elements (known as *Panchabhoota* in Sanskrit) are expressions of the same Cosmic energy, which we may call the Divine, God, or *Parashakti*.

Man himself
(the microcosm or *atman*) reflects these qualities of the universe (the macrocosm or *brahman*). Man too draws from these five major energies; he too is made of these five elements. He arises from these elements, lives in these elements and ultimately returns to these elements.

Naturally, throughout life, man longs to return to his original source, to 'return home'. So he tries to attune himself to these major energies.

Religion is nothing but the process of creating a communion between man and these vital energies.

The grossest form of cosmic energy is that of *earth*. In Man, it is represented by our body itself. As the first step towards attuning himself to the Divine, man seeks out a connection with the earth in the form of earthen idols, created in his own shape.

Man needs this 'form' to help him commune with the Divine.

For a beginner on the spiritual journey, it is difficult to even conceive of the Divine in the abstract. When it is given a form, the Divine is crystallised into something he understands and can relate to. With an idol, he can commune with the Divine in the language that he is famiIar with.

The hundreds of Hindu deities are nothing but expressions of the Divine. And yet anyone can talk to them, pray to or play with them, seek solace or give thanks. The whole awesome, indefinable nature of the Divine is scaled down to comforting proportions in the form of the deity. It *has* to be this way; the Divine without form is simply too terrifying a concept for the ordinary mind.

At a deeper, subtler level, there is one more message being reinforced - the idol before you is cast in the same form as yours, and yet it is divine. What does that say about *you*? Think about it!

So idols are definitely necessary and helpful as a 'first step', a springing board into spirituality.

As you grow spiritually, as you enter into meditation, you will be able to commune beautifully with the Divine even without any physical form in front of you. Just as children stop playing with dolls as they grow older, you will drop the idols on your own when the time comes. This is the ultimate aim of religion!

* * * * *

Q. Swamiji, why do you wear a saffron robe?

This is a question that I have to answer at least ten times every day! Especially in India, where the colour saffron has become deeply associated with orthodox Hinduism, my saffron robe (actually it's an ochre robe) attracts a lot of questions from skeptics, especially modern youngsters.

Have you heard of an emerging field called *colour therapy*?

Colour therapy is based on the fact that colours have subtle qualities that can deeply impact your mental state. Whether you realize it or not, different colours can generate different thoughts and emotions.
There is a definite scientific explanation for this:
What we call the colour of an object is nothing but the wavelength of light that it reflects. Since we ourselves have an invisible electromagnetic field around us (what is known as the 'aura' or 'plasma body'), our own magnetic field reacts with the waves of different colours to create a flux or reaction, which we interpret as 'sensations' or 'emotions'. For instance, when the wavelength of a colour and the frequency of a person's field 'match' each other, it produces a feeling of harmony and peace.

Different people react to colours in different ways, but there are many general similarities. The Luscher Colour Test developed in Basel maps 25 colours, and shows that most people pick out the same colours as having definite 'personalities'.

85

These reactions are not just emotional; we can see physiological changes also. Very often, it is a physical change in the body that causes us to interpret a colour as 'dangerous', 'calming', 'happy' and so on. When exposed to the colour red, most people show an increase in respiration rate, heartbeat and blood pressure so naturally, we think of red as 'exciting' or 'dangerous'. When exposed to pure blue, the body reacts in exactly the opposite way, and of course, blue is commonly experienced as a calming colour. Every mother knows that if her baby has trouble sleeping, a blue nightlamp in the room can help the baby (and the mother!) sleep much better. That's how certain colours have become traditionally associated with certain qualities or emotions.

Without giving it a name, we have been practising colour therapy for centuries!

In India, everything from food to human nature is classified based on its innate qualities into three types: *sattvic* (tranquil), *rajasic* (active) or *tamasic* (disruptive). Colours also can be classified in the same way: the colour red, for example, is a *rajasic* colour. It stimulates activity in the brain. That's why red is the colour of danger and love!

White is a *sattvic* colour. When you wear white, the energy flow is beautiful. The colour white has the power to make you more tranquil and receptive. White helps you absorb information more effectively. That's why, the world over, white is the preferred colour for school uniforms!

Likewise, the colour saffron (ochre) has the power to create silence in your mind. It stimulates your vital energy and creates a meditative state of mind, not only in the wearer but also in the beholders. This is the reason saffron has been traditionally worn by spiritual masters in India. It has nothing to do with Hinduism!

Be very clear: all these ancient rituals have a certain scientific basis to them. Rituals are the distillation of centuries of wisdom and the *tapas* (spiritual efforts) of innumerable enlightened masters. Rituals have lost their credibility today only because their true meaning has been lost upon the masses over time. Only the shell of the ritual remains; the spirit has departed.

Today, science itself agrees that certain colours, sounds and actions can deeply impact your state of mind, activate desired areas of the brain, and expand your consciousness. To disregard the significance of rituals, just because you cannot understand the science behind them, is like refusing to acknowledge the existence of bacteria simply because you have not seen them yourself!

So even if they seem irrelevant to you today, never underestimate the true potential of rituals. When performed in the proper way, rituals have tremendous power to bring about unimaginable levels of awareness and change.

NOTHING MYSTERIOUS AGAIN!

TRADITION DEMYSTIFIED

NOTHING MYSTERIOUS AGAIN!
TRADITION DEMYSTIFIED

Q. Swamiji, is vegetarianism necessary for leading a spiritual life?

Yes!

Now you are going to be thinking, Why?

If I say that I talk on the strength of my own experience, it won't be easy for you to believe me, because our minds have got accustomed to demanding 'scientific proof' for everything.

We manage to accept concepts like Einstein's 'spacetime' or the theories of Quantum Physics, even though we have never encountered (and never will encounter) these phenomena in our daily lives. Purely because tests have been made in a laboratory somewhere, and some statistics (which you can't understand) have been produced to support them, you feel compelled to believe.

In fact, the greatest truths of our universe cannot be proved by science; they are beyond science. Even Einstein, and most modern quantum physicists, will agree to that!

Anyway, let me give you a scientific explanation of the advantages of vegetarianism in spiritual life.

To understand this, you must first understand something about the way the human brain works.

The brain registers activity in terms of minute electric currents. When it receives information, or performs certain tasks, it generates electric currents of different frequencies or rhythms. These currents are called brain waves.

There are 4 basic kinds of brain waves, corresponding to different activities:

delta waves (produced during deep sleep), alpha waves (produced during meditation), theta waves (produced during periods of strong emotion) and beta waves (produced when the frontal lobe of the brain is stimulated, during complex mathematical or analytical activity).

Alpha waves induce a feeling of peace, tranquility and relaxed concentration that is typical of meditation and even telepathy. So all meditation techniques, whether consciously or unconsciously, try to create the right conditions for the production of alpha waves in the brain.

The strange thing about alpha waves is, they are produced by the brain at times when the oxygen supply to the brain is low. Normally we assume that lower oxygen supply will lower brain activity. But the fact is, during low-oxygen periods, the brain goes into overdrive. The blood vessels in the brain dilate to allow more blood inflow, and this creates a feeling of relaxation. Simultaneously, the brain starts producing 'relaxing' alpha waves.

So one main condition for alpha wave production is lower oxygen supply to the brain. Contrary to what we think, this doesn't affect the brain adversely in any way.

Now coming to food.

Meat is highly acidic in nature, and directly increases blood acidity. To compensate for this, the lungs take in lesser carbon-dioxide (which is also acidic) and take in more oxygen instead. So the blood reaching the brain will also have more oxygen and less carbon-dioxide.

By contrast, vegetables reduce the acidity of blood. To maintain the pH balance (acid-alkali balance) in the blood, the lungs take in more acidic carbon-dioxide. So the blood reaching the brain will also have less oxygen.

This creates the perfect condition for the brain to start producing alpha waves, which help in meditation.

This is also why high altitudes with lower oxygen levels (eg. the Himalayas) have been preferred by *rishis* (sages) since ancient times.

Of course, very few people are aware of the science behind vegetarianism. You don't need to know it, you can automatically feel the difference with a vegetarian diet.

Once you start meditating regularly, your body becomes gradually refined, becomes more fit for meditation. Then, just like your body knows which food to avoid when you have a stomach upset, it will naturally drop the foods which stop you from meditating properly.

But I say to you, don't force vegetarianism on yourself, even if you are going to take up meditation.

If you do that, the repressed desires will grow stronger and you simply won't be able to come out of their influence.

If you can drop meat without much trouble, do it.

Otherwise go ahead and enjoy it without worries or guilt. Please don't feel guilty about it!

Ultimately, the guilt can cause more energy blockages in your system; it can do more harm than the meat!

When your body is ready, it will drop the habit on its own.

* * * * *

Q. Is fasting really beneficial for health?

Yes.

Done in the right way, fasting is definitely beneficial.

Fasting has become more and more important in our time because of our eating habits, which are getting worse day by day!

Don't think fasting is done just for religious purposes. Behind all these traditions there are definite scientific reasons.

In Sanskrit we say *Annam Brahma*, Food is God.

Food is the energy which sustains our lives. Eating should be like a form of worship.

But how do we normally treat our stomach? We just keep throwing anything and everything into it! No other animal eats more than 2-3 kinds of food. In fact, other than our domesticated animals, the others just eat one kind of food throughout their lives. The lion eats only meat, the deer eats only grass. Whatever nutrition they need is supplied by that one food.

Not only that, every other animal eats only what is necessary for it at that point of time. Greed is unheard-of in the animal world!

If you notice babies, they won't drink a single drop of milk more than they need, no matter how much you force them! But we are totally deaf to the warning signals given by our stomach. Not only do we dump all kinds of food into it, we also eat much more than necessary. We treat our stomachs like a garbage dump for food!

What is the purpose of food? To give us energy.

But do we normally feel energetic after eating? NO! Usually we would all love to have a good nap after eating! To say that we feel sleepy after eating, is like saying that it grows dark when the sun rises! It is completely unnatural.

What are we doing wrong?

We are choking our system with food!

The energy used up in digestion is more than the energy released by the food. So after eating, we actually become low on energy!

The digestive energy in our body is known as jataraagni, the basic fire.

Of the five major elements *(panchabhootas)*, fire, is the meeting-point of matter and energy. Fire is that *shakti* (force) which transforms matter into energy.

On normal days, when we tax our stomachs by excessive and careless eating, the entire energy of the *jataraagni* is used up in digesting this food and cleansing the body of toxins. It is caught up with 'maintenance work'. We don't give the jataraagni a chance to perform its other important duties.

Jataraagni is a great cleansing force. When we practise fasting, jataraagni not only burns away the excess fat from our bodies, but also cleanses the negative energy which we have accumulated.

Just as poor eating habits can cause fat deposits to accumulate in our physical bodies, our suppressed emotions form a layer in our energy bodies. And over the years, just as cholesterol blocks the arteries and disrupts the blood flow in the heart, 'energy blocks' disturb the free flow of energy throughout our body.

On the days when we give the stomach rest, jataraagni is available to dissolve these energy blocks and convert the negative energy into positive energy.

That's why, when you are fasting, you usually feel more light and energetic, not tired! Just try it and see for yourself. In fact, healing and meditation will give you better results on days when you are fasting. Only if you are suffering from diabetes or acidity, it will be better to consult your doctor before deciding on fasting.

The actual days on which you fast don't matter; it's just a matter of social convention. Fasting on a particular day is followed because it's easier to keep track and be regular (e.g. every Friday or every full moon day).

But fasting at least once a fortnight is an excellent way of cleansing the body. Total fasting (drinking only water) is best, but if you can't manage that, at least try a juice or fruit diet.

It's not as difficult as it sounds! After the first few hours of intense hunger, the hunger fades on its own. And don't worry, nothing will happen to you, you won't die!

Do you know, a healthy man can survive up to 90 days on just water; our body contains enough energy reserves for 90 days. I am only asking you to give your stomach a break for 24 hours!

No Thank You!

Don't say it, feel it

No Thank You!
Don't say it, feel it

All your life, you use the words Thank You.

Right from childhood, you are taught to say Thank You. By the time we grow into adults, it has become a part of us. We use the words mechanically, in a businesslike way.

The words Thank you rarely carry the emotion that they are supposed to: gratitude.

In fact, we base our whole life on the opposite emotion: expectation.

In our relationships, we demand love. In society, we demand attention. From ourselves, we demand better and better performance. And from God, we demand everything that no one else can give us!

We keep on asking, demanding - without giving thanks for what we already have.

Gratitude is not some kind of morality which is imposed upon you.

It is a basic principle for your own happiness!

As long as you keep wanting, you are under the control of external events. When you live in gratitude, no one or nothing else can touch your happiness.

When you live with expectations, there is bound to be a gap between your expectations and their fulfillment. The moment one desire is satisfied, ten more will spring up.

Of course, in everyone's life, there will be some ups and downs. There will always be some unfulfilled desires. It is natural. As they say, it's simply a question of whether you choose to see the glass as half full or half empty!

As long as you focus on what you don't have, you will sense a vacuum in your life. The words, 'I want…' is like a black hole. It is sure to swallow up whatever you already have in your life, and leave you feeling empty.

Once a man went to Ramana Maharishi and said, Bhagwan, I want peace!

Ramana replied, From your own statement, just remove the word 'I', remove the word 'want' and what remains is Peace!

Remove the ego, remove the expectation, and peace is already yours.

You have heard the story of Shiva and the Brahma Kapala. This Brahma Kapala is inside all of us. It is nothing but our own ego.

The ego is such that it swallows everything!

In your own life, just think of the things you are wishing for right now. Make a list.

Now make a list of the things you already have. Which list makes you happy, and which list makes you uneasy?

The answer is obvious.

So which list should you be focusing on? Every living thing has the sense to focus on preserving its own happiness! Why don't we?

Whether you want to base your life on asking, or on gratitude, is entirely up to you.

There are only two kinds of religion in the world: religions based on prayer, and religions based on gratitude.

The religion of prayer can be followed by the masses. The religion of gratitude can be followed only by a select few. With prayer comes supplication, expectation. With gratitude comes spirituality.

That is the principle behind Sufism, behind Hasidism. It is the art of living in gratitude, the art of living life in such a way that everything becomes holy. The Sufis and Bhavuls sing and dance to express their gratitude to Existence. Singing and dancing is a form of prayer for them.

Showing your gratitude is not a matter of spending hours doing pooja. Just being joyful, being aware of the gift of life, is enough.

Showing gratitude has become such a ritual, such a duty for us, that we have forgotten what real gratitude feels like.

All your life you are taught to be grateful to your parents, to your teachers, to friends and strangers. This is just a conditioning! When real gratitude arises, you will see what a tremendous difference there is! Gratitude is nothing but an upsurge of joy, of compassion. It flows from you without your awareness; you can't help it!

We have not tasted the sweetness of gratitude, the tremendous sense of fulfillment that you feel when you pay your gratitude to Existence.

A small story:

> The Sufi master Junnaid used to pay his gratitude to God five times every day. At one time, he and his followers were wandering through some villages where Sufism was not accepted.
>
> In the first village, people refused to give them alms, so they were forced to go without food that day. The next day, the same thing happened. On the third day, the village they passed through was so hostile that they were driven out with sticks and stones.
>
> That night as usual, Junnaid knelt down and offered his gratitude to God. Seeing this, some of his disciples were furious.
>
> For three days we have gone without food, Master! Today we were driven out of that village like dogs! Is this what you are offering your gratitude for? they questioned him.
>
> Junnaid replied, I never used to thank Existence for anything in particular! I never felt grateful for any reason. Then how can I stop being grateful for any reason? My gratitude doesn't need reasons; it simply flows.

Life itself is a great gift from Existence.

Living itself is enough reason to be grateful. Existence is showering on us! The sunshine, the flowers, your body, your life; did you ask for any of these?

Have we worked very hard to deserve life?

Can anyone say that they have spent time in God's kitchen or garden, labouring hard so that they are granted this life?

No!

Life has simply been gifted to us.

That's why we value it so cheaply, that's why we take life for granted.

In the beginning, all religions, all cultures used to emphasize gratitude to Life. But gradually, we have forgotten it. In India, we have the phrase, Annam Brahma (Food is God). Christians and Jews say grace before every meal. But how often do we really feel the gratitude? Usually we just mumble the words out of habit.

One of my devotees told me this story; this really happened:

He used to call his wife from office every afternoon at lunchtime.

Just before hanging up, he always used to tell her, I love you.

One day, his boss called him on the phone at lunchtime. After speaking, he said without thinking, I love you! And unfortunately for him, his boss was a lady! You can imagine what happened after that.

This is what happens when you just act out of habit, without internalizing the meaning of the words. Just as this man used to say I love you casually, without really feeling any love, we also say Thank you without any true sense of gratitude.

In Tantra, before making love, the two people worship each other, because they are going to enter into the merging of two divine energies. They welcome each other with reverence and gratitude.

That is the difference between Sex, Love and Compassion!

This doesn't apply to your relationships alone. It is an evaluation of your attitude towards life itself.

When you give and take with only expectation, and no respect, your relationship with life will be like sex. It is bound to result in short-term pleasure, and long-term frustration.

When you give and take with expectation, but also with respect, then it is Love. This is the way most of us live. We respect life, but we also get hurt when life doesn't give us what we want.

With compassion, there is no expectation; only a free and joyful giving. Like the flower spreads its fragrance without thinking about whether it will be appreciated or not, we just give love out of the overflowing of compassion.

And don't think that if you give without expecting, you will get nothing in return! It is exactly the opposite. When you live in gratitude, you will be blessed by Life.

In compassion, you are grateful that the other accepts what you give, helps you share, eases the burden of your love. Have you ever thought about that? Not to be loved is very difficult, but not being allowed to love is far worse! If someone doesn't return your love, you can bear it. But if someone doesn't even accept your love, can you bear it? We are all born to give; we are just not aware of it.

In India, we have a beautiful concept that is unheard of in the West: in India, it is the giver who says thank you!

This is because, the other has given him a chance to give, has accepted his offering. In India it is considered a sin to take, and a privilege to give. So the giver thanks the taker for doing him a favour, for accepting his offering. But I say, when you give and accept without expectation, both become sacred acts. As Shakespeare says so beautifully about compassion; both he who gives and he who receives are blessed.

The only way to have a live connection with reality, with Existence, is through gratitude.

When you are loving, flowing, filled with gratitude, you will always feel the tremendous energy of Existence flow through you.

Don't say thank you, be a thank you!

Don't pay gratitude, become gratitude!

This is Tathata - accepting whatever life gives you with reverence and gratitude.

Gratitude is the most effortless path to lifelong happiness.
Thank you!

WHAT IS *KARMA*?

UNDERSTANDING THE LAW

WHAT IS *KARMA*?
UNDERSTANDING THE LAW

Karma is among the most popular and the least understood of Eastern philosophical concepts! Today, even in the West, almost everyone thinks he has a pretty good idea of what karma is.

But what most of them think is, karma is a grand philosophy that needs to be expounded upon through hundreds of pages.

Actually, karma is nothing but the simple law of cause and effect.

Karma is a law of nature, like the force of gravity or electricity.

If you drop a brick on your foot, you are going to get hurt. But do you think of that as a punishment for dropping the brick? NO!

It's a cause and effect relationship; simple.

Karma works exactly this way. Karma is the natural result of certain actions performed by you at an earlier time. Like the Bible says, as you sow, so you reap.

The only difference is, karma is a kind of 'delayed effect'.

Karma also works across lifetimes; which means that, the cause may exist in one life, but the result may be experienced in the next or later lives. This naturally raises the question, Does reincarnation really happen? But we will discuss that another time, not now!

Being human, we naturally cannot remember the cause that has happened in a previous lifetime. Because of our own limited vision, we perceive only the result, and can't understand why this is happening.

From primitive times, whenever something happens which is beyond our understanding, we attribute it to punishment by the Gods. Even today, in many civilizations, natural calamities like floods and earthquakes are seen as punishments imposed on us by angry Gods. That's why a moral angle has been given to karma. It is society that is entirely responsible for explaining karma as a punishment for the 'sins' of a previous life. In a way, this is also a kind of coping technique. It is easier to bear some misfortune in your life if you feel that your own evil act (in a previous lifetime) must be responsible for it.

The concept of sin and punishment itself is created only by society, partly for its own efficient functioning. If people are not afraid of punishment, society can degenerate into a state of lawlessness. The truth is, we are not punished for our sins. We are punished by our sins! Every 'sin' brings its own punishment with it. It's a package deal! Every time you get angry, just watch your body. Your pulse starts racing, your BP goes up, your body gets into a state of stress from which it can take hours to recover. Not only that, you usually end up feeling guilty about it afterwards. Nobody else needs to punish you for getting angry. Your anger itself is punishing you enough!

If you drink too much, you are going to suffer from liver cirrhosis. You are not being punished by some external force for drinking; you are being punished by your drinking habit itself; if you are intelligent enough to perceive it as your punishment.

To a doctor, of course, it is simply the natural result of alcoholism.

Karma operates in the same way. The reason that it is more difficult to understand is, karma doesn't work only on the physical plane, like a falling brick. Karma works on the mental, emotional, even the spiritual plane.

Suppose you are unable to fulfill a particular desire in one life, or suppose you are forced to leave some action incomplete, the unfulfilled desire or unfinished act creates a kind of emotional or mental vacuum in your life. That vacuum can act as a suction force and draw you to fulfill the same desire or repeat the same act in the next life.

So at the emotional and mental level, karma is the sum total of all your unfulfilled desires and incomplete actions - the baggage from a previous life.

And every life, you work out the karmas of a previous life, but keep on adding fresh desires or fresh unfulfilled actions to your current baggage which will become the karmas of your next life. That's why karma is an endless cycle.

What is the way out of karma?

As long as we live, there is no escape from karma, because to live is to have desires, and we certainly can't fulfill all our desires in one lifetime. But it is in your hands to drastically reduce the effects of karma - by awakening your consciousness. By understanding the true nature of karma, and how it works, we can find a way out.

Sri Ramakrishna tells a beautiful story which will give you intellectual clarity on the subject. Of course, no one can give you existential, experiential clarity on karma as it really is that clarity comes only with enlightenment. And when you are enlightened, you cannot express it!

Coming to the story on karma:

Our state is similar to that of a cow tied to a post with a long rope. Inside that perimeter, it can sit, stand, feed, do whatever it pleases. The same with us! It is true that karma creates certain bondage, gives our life certain direction, forces us to act in certain ways. We have a limited amount of freedom; the rest is in the hands of Existence. But Ramakrishna also adds, if we use our freedom intelligently, it is possible that Existence will extend our rope, or even free us completely. You can choose whether to remain in bondage or work towards being set free.

Karma is closely related to Dharma.

Dharma is another much-misunderstood word. Dharma is usually interpreted as 'duty', but that is totally wrong. That is also a social, moralistic interpretation. The closest translation of dharma is 'true nature'. For example, it is the dharma (nature) of fire to burn. Similarly, it is the dharma of water to be wet. If water tries to burn, something unnatural is happening.

As long as you act according to your dharma, you cannot attract karma. In simple words, be natural. Function according to your true nature.

Seems easy doesn't it? But it is not so for us because of all our conditioning!

This is the toughest thing to do - because we cannot identify what our true nature is! In life, we take on the character and desires of everybody around us and finally we can't recognize which is truly ours and which is borrowed.

It's like this: let us say, you need to buy a television. When you go to the supermarket, you find someone else buying a washing machine, another person buying a refrigerator, another buying a music system. And you are tempted to acquire all these things as well! Without realizing, you take on the desires of all the people around you. In one life, you try to fulfill the desires of hundreds of people. These desires are not natural to you; they are acquired desires. So naturally, they attract karma.

All karma arises from ignorance; from ignorance of your true nature.

In terms of spirituality, karma is determined by the dominant quality of your life.

Spirituality is nothing but the science of awakening your consciousness, of realizing your true nature. When your whole life is directed towards awakening your consciousness, you will naturally not fall into the trap of ignorance. With clarity and awareness, you can identify which are your true desires, which is your true nature.

This becomes especially significant at the moment of Death.

In fact, in yoga, in Zen, all meditation is nothing but a preparation for the moment of death. If you are in a state of consciousness at the time of death, you will enter into your next life also in a conscious way, not in ignorance. When you enter into life with awareness, you ensure that you live your life in awareness, creating as little karma as possible.

This is true.

I speak to you from the authority of my own experience.

I speak to you from the explosion of awareness that has happened inside me.

Someday, you will know it yourself.

Awaken your consciousness, and you are taking the first step that will ultimately free you from karma.

WHAT IS YOUR *MANTRA*?
A POWER BEYOND WORDS

WHAT IS YOUR *MANTRA?*
A POWER BEYOND WORDS

Q. Swamiji, do mantras really have power?

Yes, mantras (sacred chants) have tremendous power, but not in the way people think!

Mantras are powerful, but not because they somehow manage to convince the Gods of wealth or knowledge to bestow favours upon us.

Mantras are effective because they are a carefully arranged sequence of sounds, and sound is a powerful form of energy.

What we perceive as different sounds are actually vibrations of different frequencies. Our ears pick up these vibrations and the brain 'translates' them as sounds.

When sound waves follow one another in a regular sequence, it creates a sense of harmony, which we call music. When it is an irregular pattern, we call it 'noise'.

Words are nothing but sounds to which we have given some meaning. On the energy level, they still function just as waves, as vibrations. Like colours, different vibrations can stimulate different physical and emotional reactions in you. This is because of the property of resonance. When sound waves of a certain frequency meet with your brain waves, the combination can create either a harmonious or a disharmonious effect; or they can activate or 'put to sleep' different areas of the brain. This can affect you both physiologically and emotionally.

Do you know, the Samurai warriors of Japan use the 'fighting cry' or *kiai* for exactly this effect?

When this sound is produced in a minor key, it has the power to lower the arterial BP and instantly create partial paralysis in the opponent! Simultaneously, it also activates the 'fear' area of the brain and creates a sense of panic in the opponent's mind.

So be very clear: words are not just words! They are embodiments of sound energy.

Mantras work in exactly the same way.

Chanting the Saraswati stotram regularly is said to help students in doing well in their studies. Why? It's not as if Saraswati (the Goddess of learning) is going to appear before them and grant them a boon that they will pass in their exams!

The fact is, the bija mantra (sacred syllable) in the Saraswati stotram, when repeated continuously, has been proved to stimulate the areas of the brain which control memory power and concentration. Repeating this mantra is like giving that part of the brain a vigorous warm-up exercise! So naturally, a student who chants this mantra before taking up his books can concentrate better and remember his lesson far more effectively.

Devoted worshippers sometimes claim that they can invoke the form of a particular deity just by chanting the appropriate mantra. I myself have experienced this many times when I perform powerful yagas or homas (rituals based on making offerings to agni, the fire energy). During the ritual, the sacred fire actually takes the shape of the deity that is invoked with the mantra. Plenty of photographs exist to prove this phenomenon.

It may sound like magic, but there is a sound scientific reason for this.

Have you heard of the tonoscope?

In the late 20th century, an experimenter in Switzerland called Hans Jenny invented an instrument called the tonoscope. This instrument can convert sounds into graphical patterns. If a person speaks into the instrument, it can create a 'picture' of what he said, depending on the sounds of the words!

When they tested the tonoscope, the experimenters were surprised. They found that when someone spoke the sound 'Ohhh' into the tonoscope, the picture that came out would be a perfect circle an 'O'! The vibrations produced by the sound 'Ohhh', when represented graphically, naturally take the shape of the circle that we use to represent it in written language.

That means there is a definite relationship between the sound and the form it takes. Different vibrations appear to our eyes as certain forms. When a particular mantra is chanted, a vibration is set up in the fire, which causes it to take a certain wave-like shape. It is from this shape that the earliest Hindu seers initially drew out the rough form of the deity. So naturally, anyone who chants the same series of sounds perfectly will be able to set up the same vibration, and ultimately see the same shape, or 'deity' in the fire. Simple!

Without our awareness, mantras work on us in many subtle ways. On the energy level, mantras work as catalysts or 'purifiers'. This concept is a little more difficult to understand, but I can tell you from my experience that it is true.

You have three energies in your system: Ichcha shakti (the power of visualization), Kriya shakti (the power of action) and Gnana shakti (the power of knowledge). Iccha shakti is the 'base metal' from which the other two energies can be created by the process of purification.

When added into your energy (your force-field) repeatedly, the vibrations of mantras have the power to process ichcha shakti and purify it to Gnana shakti.

The word mantra can mean two things:

Man-tra: Man means mankind, tra means that which shows the way. So mantra is that which shows the way to man.

Man-tra: Man also means mind, tra means that which shows the way, so mantra could also mean that which shows the way out of the mind, which brings you out of the mind.

When mantras are added to your being continuously, like acid is added to the raw material to cleanse it, your being becomes like 22 carat gold.

If you continue the process, it will ultimately become 24 carat gold. So mantras are powerful techniques to enter into the spiritual zone which I call the real life.

But we don't just use mantras in the spiritual life. We are all chanting mantras continuously, whether we are religious or non-religious, spiritual or materialistic. Every single day in our daily lives, we use mantras without even being aware of it. It is not necessary that the mantra should be in Sanskrit. Don't think mantra means Om Namah Shivaya, or Hari Om Namoh Narayana. You can use even English mantras: I must win! , I must convince that person! I must make her love me! These mantras acquire their power not from their sound, but from the energy you have invested in them.

But you don't realize the power of these mantras!

A small story:

Once, a famous oriental speaker was giving a talk in the West about the significance of mantras. A man stood up and challenged him,

I don't believe this nonsense. How can repeating a string of words have any effect on our minds? Are we so foolish?

The speaker glared at him and roared, SHUT UP, YOU STUPID IDIOT! HOW DARE YOU CHALLENGE ME!

The man who asked the question was simply furious. He started trembling in anger, and started showering abuse on the speaker, threatening to report him to the police, and so on.

When the man finally finished, the speaker started laughing, and told him,

If a few words uttered by a stranger can have such a disruptive impact on your conscious mind, how can you doubt that positive statements, consciously and continuously repeated to yourself, can have an impact on your unconscious mind?

Whatever words you repeat continuously, whatever message you feed your unconscious with, can become a mantra for you. Whatever you utter can become a mantra!

In fact, that is the way you attain something. Any desire in your life, first appears only in the form of a wish, a mantra. With continuous effort, you convert it into reality.

But be very clear: if the mantra is unconscious, the result is also 'unconscious', not in your control. If the mantra is chanted in awareness, if you direct your energy with a proper sense of purpose, the result will also be as you desire.

How do you know whether a mantra is conscious or unconscious?

Examine closely the forces that are driving you in daily life. Are you aware of what they are and how they are influencing your actions? Are you consciously following a certain path? Are you clear why?

When your mantra is unconscious, when you are repeating actions because of a habit pattern that you don't understand, you have no control of the result. Your life will be dragged wherever these unconscious impulses take it.

If you decide to chant the mantra consciously, you will be driving the car. If you let the mantra chant you, if you let the unconscious process continue in you and control your actions, the car will be driving you!

If you drive the car, you know where you are going. If the car drives you, you have no idea where you will reach or whether you will reach!

So flood your mind with your consciousness.

Choose your mantra with clarity and commitment.

Then, the path and the goal will both become clear to you.

You will reach your goal dancing!

WHAT IS THE
BIG HURRY?
TAKE LIFE IN SMALL DOSES

WHAT IS THE BIG HURRY?
TAKE LIFE IN SMALL DOSES

The other day I came across an advertisement in a magazine.
It was for a painkiller - a headache pill, or something of that sort:
A modern young woman smiled at me confidently from the ad.
The ad said:

> 6 am - wake up
> 8 am - kids
> 9 am - office
> 11 am - meeting
> 1 pm - business lunch
> 6 pm - traffic
> 7 pm - groceries
> 8 pm - guests
> 10 pm - (name of pill)

The woman was smiling as if it was the most natural thing in the world to have a headache pill every night before bed. It was so beautifully conveyed!

What sort of life is this to be leading? To be running from morning to night, from one day to the next! No wonder she has a headache every night!

And the worst thing is, this pace of life has become totally normal, totally accepted today. It has become totally normal to be in a desperate hurry, rushing through life.

Just stop on the road and watch the traffic at a signal.

Everybody is busy tooting their horns for no reason in particular.

And the instant the lights change, if one unfortunate person isn't able to start his car on time, there will be a hundred people honking him off the road.

Hurry seems to be the peculiar disease of our time.

Machines are being invented every day to do work faster and faster. The fastest computers perform thousands of operations every second.

Supersonic jets carry us from one place to another at speeds greater than the speed of sound.

Communication networks transmit information at tremendous speeds across continents, via satellites stationed far above the earth.

As they say, we have communication @ the speed of thought!

But where are we going in such a hurry?

Where are we all running to?

Or rather, what are we all running away from?

The truth is, we are running towards and running away from.

We are driven by two equally compelling reasons: Greed and Fear.

Greed tells us: there is no time! In the span of sixty or seventy years granted to you, you need to live out so many desires! You need to possess the maximum number of things, you need to taste the maximum number of experiences.

You need to live life with a vengeance!

Like a terminally ill patient determined to enjoy the last couple of months of his life, we rush from pleasure to pleasure endlessly.

And every day, we come under fresh assaults from the media.

When you are going to work, just read the hoardings on the road. They are all saying the same thing!

When you go home, switch on the television and watch the ads.

What are they saying? The same thing!

Every hour of the day, we are being told that our life would be incomplete without a new job, a new car, a new girlfriend, a new home.

Where is the time to acquire all that we need? So we start running.

We have to earn, we have to prove ourselves!

And since we have so little time, we have to lead multiple lives.

We try to cram 48 hours, 72 hours into each day. Ultimately, we have to cram several lifetimes into one!

But physically, there is a limit to what we can do in one day. We can only be in one place at a time. So we begin to live part of our lives cerebrally with our minds.

This is the latest way of living our lives!

Cerebral enjoyment is nothing but enjoying without really enjoying.

The software engineer working till 3am or 4am in his office in the city is sure to have on his computer desktop a beautiful picture of mountains or a beach!

Sitting in his office, he watches and enjoys the beauty of the mountains; he tries to listen to the waves on the beach.

What is this called..? There's a word... Multitasking? According to the engineer, he is multitasking! Working in his office, he is also enjoying on the beach. A smart choice!

But the sad truth is, the picture on his desktop represents the holiday he will never have the time to take. Because he is too busy working, too busy aiming at that miraculous promotion that will make him the company's youngest project manager, years ahead of his time.

We are obsessed with the idea of finishing things before their time.

These days, we try to toilet-train six-month-old babies!

We expect our children to grow up years faster than their time.

It is as absurd as expecting a mango tree to bear fruit in the very first year! It simply goes against the nature of the tree.

Why do we do this?

In earlier times, one lifetime seemed perfectly sufficient to do whatever one desired in life.

After all, what did a man want? After some amount of education, he would continue to look after his father's fields or his business. He would get married, produce children and live out his life in the same town, in the same house. Where was the hurry?

Now, we no longer have the patience to live life as it comes!

A few weeks ago, a young man came to see me. He must have been in his mid-thirties, working in a private firm.

He told me,

I've got everything settled, Swamiji.

I'm building a house for which I've taken a 25-year loan. By the time the loan is paid up, my daughter will be married and settled (his daughter was a little girl who was holding his hand). My son would also be settled in a job (his wife was carrying an infant boy in her arms). By then the land would have appreciated in the area where we're building our house. So we can sell it out. My wife can take VRS (voluntary retirement) which will fetch us some additional benefits. After settling some amount on our grandchildren, we can invest the rest and then settle down in your ashram. Definitely we'll be coming to the ashram Swamiji. Our life is with you only!

Just imagine!

In the five minutes that he talked to me, the man had finished with 25 years of his life! He was in such a hurry, he had extracted the juice out of those 25 years by thinking about it, by planning it all ahead of time. Now what was left for living was just the dried-up skin called life.

And he was telling me that his sole interest in life was spirituality except for the call of duty which was forcing him to carry on his life in this way.

Tell me, is this a spiritual way of living life, mortgaging the present to the future?

Loans and credit cards are nothing but ways of trying to live tomorrow's life today. We spend today the money that we are going to earn tomorrow!

While still in the present, we manage to live our future. Is that possible? It's a reversal of time that would interest Einstein!

Our lives are a constant running towards the future. Whatever is available today is never sufficient, never good enough for us.

This is a relatively new phenomenon, especially in the East. For centuries, we have been used to thinking of this life as a 'passing phase'. The idea of reincarnation, of a cycle of birth and death, was built so strongly into our minds that people would think,

So what if we don't fulfill all our desires this time? There's always another life!

Whereas Hurry, like science and technology, is a gift of the West.

Naturally, because in the West people do not believe in more than one life.

In fact, hurry is just negative fallout of the positive discipline of science. Science helps us live life at its optimum. Technology helps us get the maximum out of this life. In terms of psychology, we could say science is the extroverted, outward-looking part of ourselves.

Science is consciousness spiraling outward. Science aims at accumulating knowledge, at achieving results, at doing things faster and better. Without science, we would still be in the bullock-cart age!

But science carried too far results in the kind of mad hurry we see today. This constant running only reflects the restlessness we feel inside.

In fact, it is because of our inner restlessness that we feel compelled to run. We feel we are missing out on something important. We don't know what it is, but we have to hurry up and find it!

How many of us have dreamt, at some time or the other, of missing an important train or bus?

This is a very common dream, and very significant.

It shows that most of us are living in fear of having missed out on life.

Deep inside, we sense that somehow we have missed the train of life.

And we can't understand how it has happened!

Throughout the dream we are hurrying, hurrying, checking the timetable, making plans, screaming to each other to hurry up. But when we finally make it to the station, the train is already leaving. It is too late!

These days, we even have simultaneous bookings on five different trains; so many backup plans, yet we find that we have somehow missed them all.

This is exactly what happens in our lives.

Our behaviour today is like a child who is given ten lollipops of different flavours, and only five minutes to eat them! We take greedy licks out of each of them, but have no time to truly savour any of the flavours.

Just for a moment, turn around and see clearly how you have led your life in the past five years.

How often have you given up doing things that you really wanted to do simply because there was no time?

Was all the running worth it?

Understand, I don't mean that it is alright to lead our lives in philosophical lethargy - the custom in the East!

It does not mean postponing life.

It is not possible to live only in the present, ignoring the future altogether.

Every day, we are called upon to take action, make decisions. We have to live with deadlines. We have to think ahead, fulfill our dreams.

Certainly, you should plan for tomorrow.

But don't forget to live today!

What I mean is, live consciously.

Live with awareness.

Learn to be present in every moment of your life.

Whatever you are doing at the moment, do it with totality.

Watch every act.

Even if it is an everyday act, do it as if you were doing it for the first time.

Of course, it is not easy. Most of the time we don't do very interesting things at least, not the things that we normally call interesting! At nine in the morning, you may be on a crowded bus on your way to work. At eight in the night, you may be finishing household tasks - like the woman in the advertisement. It doesn't matter!

Whatever you do, do it with totality.

Be very clear: this is the reality of the moment. There is no running away from it.

So you may as well enjoy it, enjoy washing the dishes or whatever you are doing! Even if you want to, you can't run two hours into the future where you are fast asleep in bed. Maybe mentally you can do it, but physically this is where you are!

Lao Tzu uses the beautiful word Wei-wu-wei.

Wei-wu-wei means action without action.

It must be the most joyous way to live!

Wei-wu-wei is to enter into each action totally, playfully, spontaneously. It is a beautiful way of transforming work into play.

The next time you are feeling miserable about washing the dishes, just call your child over and give him or her a chance!

Just watch how she does it. She washes the dishes with every cell of her little body! She enjoys every pattern the soap bubbles make on the dishes. She is in no hurry to finish it and get on with more important things in her life.

In fact, for every child, whatever she is doing at the moment is the most important thing in her life!

That is Wei-wu-wei.

So this constant discontentment with the present, the greed to cram more and more into one lifetime, is one reason why we are always in a hurry.

But greed is not the only reason!

For many of us, it is also because we are afraid to stop.

Fear is a major reason why we cling so much to the outer flow of life.

Hurrying is a way of escaping from ourselves!

To stop, to stand still for a moment, is to encounter our deepest selves. It is to come face to face with the silence and stillness inside. For minds accustomed to the constant din of the outside world, encountering this silence can be a terrifying experience.

Seriously, how many of us have the courage to face ourselves?

To look inward is to run the risk of discovering that after running and running; we haven't moved at all.

This is one reason why so many people are afraid of meditation. They come to me and say, Swamiji, what should I do to experience peace of mind?

If I tell them to go around some temple 108 times, they will do it happily. After all, that is still something that they can do running! But if I ask them to spend half an hour in meditation, that is too much.

In Zen, they have a beautiful meditation practice called just sitting.

What a name: just sitting!

Zen is the only religion today that is truly alive, truly responsive to the changing needs of each time and age.

In just sitting meditation, participants have to do just that: sit still and do nothing. Actually, all meditation is about sitting still and doing nothing, but this technique makes us do it consciously.

And nothing can be tougher for most people! All our lives we have been moving with such terrific momentum, that simply to stop, requires supreme effort.

Because to stop is to take a fresh look at our lives.

To get in touch with our forgotten selves.

To see clearly what we're doing, and why we're doing it.

(Even if it means finding out that most of the reasons we started out with don't hold good anymore.)

There is no other way!

Remember, even the best transatlantic carriers can't fly endlessly without refueling.

To hurry endlessly is a sure way to invite neurosis.

Stopping is a healing process in itself.

Stopping gives meaning to all our hurrying.

Try this fun experiment with your family or friends: tell each other when to STOP!

This is an excellent technique.

When you are in the middle of something, if someone screams, Stop! Just stop whatever you may be doing, even if it is in the middle of lifting your leg, you will be suddenly thrown back into the present!

There is a sudden pause in your hurrying.

You make a leap into awareness.

You re-enter the Now!

WHY SUFFER?

HAPPINESS IS A CHOICE

WHY SUFFER?

HAPPINESS IS A CHOICE

Q. Swamiji, what is Suffering? Is suffering essential in our lives?

There is a beautiful Buddhist *sutra*:
No suffering, no cause, no end.

What exactly is *suffering*?
Almost all of us have undergone suffering at some time of our lives.
Now suppose I ask you, *Why did you choose to suffer? Was your suffering necessary?*
You would certainly find that an absurd question!
Does anyone choose to suffer? you would ask me. *Suffering just happens to one, that's all. It can't be helped…*
But the truth is, **suffering is a choice!**
Suffering is not a state of life - it is a state of mind. It is an internal event, not an external event! Whether you suffer or not in a particular situation depends entirely on how you choose to handle that situation.
For me to tell you that your suffering was unreal would be unfair, and untrue. Because *for you*, your suffering was real, and inevitable. You never gave yourself the option of not suffering! You didn't even know you had the choice.

133

But now, consider this question consciously:

When do you undergo suffering?

When you fall ill? When your neighbour gets a new car? When your partner leaves you for someone else?

Well, suppose you decided to just accept these situations without anger or resentment. Would you still suffer as much? After all, there is nothing inherently painful about your neighbour getting a new car!

Even if there is pain in the moment, as when a loved one leaves, you cannot wish it away. By accepting the moment, instead of resisting it, you automatically bring down your level of suffering. ***Suffering is always, ALWAYS born of resistance to the present moment.*** When you stop resisting, you stop suffering!

A man who had fallen out of a second-floor window and miraculously survived, was visited in hospital by a friend.

Did the fall hurt very much?, the friend enquired politely.

Oh no, the fall was totally painless. It was only the landing that hurt!, replied the man.

As long as you go with the flow, there is no pain, no suffering. When you place *your* ideas and expectations in the way of life, you create obstacles to that flow. Often, the defenses that you set up to escape pain cause more suffering than the event itself!

Consider even Death! As an event, death can hurt you only once. But the fear of death haunts you all your life! Your constant running away from death causes you more suffering than death itself!

Suffering is rarely caused by a major event, like an accident or a fatal disease. Most of our suffering stems from the day-to-day frictions in relationships, the push and pull of daily living.

In many homes, even after 30 years of married life, you will find the husband and wife quarrelling over the same issues everyday! Neither are they able to change their own behaviour, nor are they able to accept the other's. This is what is true *samsara* worldly life; your own repetitive patterns of living, which you can neither recognize nor control, but which cause you endless suffering.

Suffering happens when you invest too much, emotionally, in other people or in external events. After all, how much control do you have over them?

Become your own source of inspiration. Don't mortgage your happiness to someone else! Remember, *you are 100% responsible for your own happiness. No one or nothing can make you suffer without your silent permission!* These are not just words to motivate you. It is the simple truth.

Try to make a habit of witnessing your own experiences. What is making you suffer in a particular situation? Is there something you can do about it?

If you *can* do something, do it.

If the situation is beyond your control, you can react in one of these ways: (a) you can allow yourself to suffer, or (b) you can accept the situation, and get on with your life.

It is your choice!

> During the last years of Sri Ramakrishna's life, even when he was afflicted with cancer, he continued to live a normal life. Physically, it was a daily battle against the disease, but the master was at peace.
>
> One day, a concerned disciple asked him, *How can you smile like this? How are you coping with so much suffering?*
>
> *What suffering?* questioned Sri Ramakrishna in return. *There is pain, but there is certainly no suffering!*

To be free of suffering does not mean there is no more pain. Life has not yet given us a remedy for cancer, starvation or stubbing your toe against the furniture. Freedom lies only in refusing the pain a reaction, in not allowing it an influence over you.

You ask me - *is suffering essential?*

Yes, in a way it is, because suffering can be a powerful catalyst to growth. Just like a seed first has to rupture before a plant can grow and blossom, intense suffering can break down the defenses of your ego, leaving you open and vulnerable to Existence. With your usual thought patterns shattered, you begin to see things as they actually are.

Pain is part of everybody's life. True maturity lies in knowing how to use that pain before it uses you!

A small story:

> Two men, one a *gnani* (a wise man), and the other an ordinary person, were traveling through a forest on a dark, moonless night.
>
> Suddenly, a shaft of lightning flashed in the sky.
>
> The ordinary man began to tremble in fear. A storm! His mind was immediately given over to confusion. *Should he walk on? Or should he find a safe place to stop till the storm was spent?* The man began wishing that he had never decided to undertake this journey. He cursed himself as foolish and unlucky. In other words, he fell headlong into suffering!
>
> The *gnani,* on the other hand, simply used the moments of lightning to take a better look at the road ahead. He ensured that he was traveling in the right direction, thanked the lightning for its help, and moved onward.

Pain is just like this flash of lightning. You have no control over its existence. But whether you suffer from it, or learn from it, is entirely up to you!

Are you enjoying suffering?

One of the most deeply hidden reasons for suffering is: you could be enjoying it. Even falling ill can become a source of pleasure if it fetches you the attention and care you have been craving for.

A small story:

> A man working in a large firm would bring the same dish for lunch everyday. Everyday he would complain about how much he hated that particular dish, and his sympathetic friends would share their lunch with him. Taking pity on the man's plight, his friends finally advised him, *Why don't you ask your wife to cook something you like, for a change? How can she not be aware that you hate this dish?*
>
> *What wife?* the man asked in surprise. *I'm a bachelor. I cook my own lunch!*

How often do you find yourself doing this - in subtle ways? Deliberately creating suffering for yourself and gain self pity and another's sympathy? For instance, going without dinner just to spite someone whom you've had a quarrel with?

Examine why it sometimes gives you pleasure to inflict pain on yourself, or on others. Is there a better channel through which you can receive the same pleasure - without the suffering? Is there a positive way to tackle your needs?

Become aware - this is the first step.

The second is to *accept totally* the Here and Now.

Awareness with acceptance - this is the only way out of suffering.

I don't mean that you needn't take steps to improve your situation. Take all the necessary steps - but don't let the situation overwhelm you.

Don't react - just act!

APPENDIX

ABOUT PARAMAHAMSA NITHYANANDA

Rare living incarnation from India, Paramahamsa Nithyananda, has emerged as a compelling spiritual force of our millennium. Working and sharing with over 20 million people worldwide every year, Nithyananda is committed to help humanity make the next big breakthrough: into Superconsciousness.

A spiritual genius with an enlightened insight into everything from management to meditation, from relationships to religion, and from success to sannyas, Nithyananda brings to us a wealth of practical wisdom, meditation techniques and tools for lasting inner transformation. Further, thousands of people have experienced healing of diseases ranging from depression to cancer, often with a single touch. Today, Nithyananda is currently the most watched spiritual master on YouTube, and the bestselling author of over 200 internationally published books in over 25 languages.

A recent survivor of religious persecution and unlawful imprisonment in his own country, Nithyananda has emerged still stronger from the attack, and continues to reveal to the world the deeper dimensions of yoga and meditation drawn from the ancient mystic disciplines of the East.

Nithyananda's authenticity, spontaneity and his deeply compassionate insight into our own struggles and aspirations make his teachings relevant across the barriers of space, time and mind.

ABOUT NITHYANANDA MISSION

The world is awakening to a new consciousness, where distinctions like material life and spiritual life, inner growth and outer growth, are rapidly breaking down. The new age individual is striving to build a harmonious world where material success complements spiritual growth, where ancient wisdom and modern scientific insights blend seamlessly to create a richer and more fulfilling life for all.

Carrying these revolutionary truths to the global community is the effort of Nithyananda Mission. Nithyananda Mission is a worldwide movement which is committed to bringing about a true awakening for all beings on our planet, irrespective of race, gender or nationality. Reinterpreting ancient Vedic wisdom in the light of modern living, the Mission creates opportunities for the powerful transformation of the individual and the community.

PROGRAMS AND WORKSHOPS

Nithyananda Dhyanapeetam offers specialized meditation programs worldwide, to benefit millions of people at the levels of body, mind and spirit. A few of them are listed below:

INNER AWAKENING

A unique and intense 21-day meditation program aimed at realizing one's full potential in all aspects of life. Some amongst its many highlights are:

- Nithya Yoga to create a yogic body,
- A diverse mix of meditation techniques to cleanse and energize one's mind and soul (including past life regression),
- Powerful energy darshans,
- Enlightening campfire sessions,

- Intense Kundalini Awakening sessions where participants experience physical levitation.

Scientifically proven to increase the mitochondrial cell energy by over 1300%, this program also offers various health benefits like blood sugar and blood pressure regulation, weight balancing and relief from insomnia to name a few.

ENWEALTH

A unique weekend workshop with Paramahamsa Nithyananda where he imparts the hidden Vedic secrets of creating wealth – such as the right inner space for attracting and managing wealth, flawless and responsible decision-making, techniques for negotiating for effortless success.

NITHYANANDA MISSION HIGHLIGHTS

- **Meditation and de-addiction camps worldwide:** Over 5 million people impacted to date

- **Nithya Spiritual Healing:** A system of cosmic energy healing administered free through 5000 ordained healers healing both mind and body

- **Anna Daan: free food program:** 10,000 nutritious meals distributed every week through all the ashram *anna mandirs* for visitors, devotees and disciples thus improving health standards

- **The Nithyananda Order and its training:** Spiritual aspirants ordained as *Sannyasis*, *Brahmacharis* and *Brahmacharinis*: who undergo years of intensive training in yoga, meditation, deep spiritual practice, Sanskrit, *vedic* chanting, life skills, and who run the 100% volunteer based ashrams of Nithyananda Dhyanapeetam worldwide, working in all Mission activities

- **Nithya Yoga:** A revolutionary system of yoga in the lines of sage Patanjali's original teachings, taught in 15 countries

- **Nithyananda Vedic Temples:** Over 33 Vedic temples and spiritual research academies worldwide

- **Meditation Programs in prisons:** Conducted in prisons and juvenile camps to reform extremist attitudes – resulting in amazing transformation among the inmates

- **Medical Camps:** Free treatment and therapies in allopathy, homeopathy, ayurveda, acupuncture, eye check-ups, eye surgeries, artificial limb donation camps, gynecology and more

- **Support to children in rural areas:** School buildings, school uniforms and educational materials provided free to rural schools

- **Nithyananda Vidyalaya:** Enlightenment based education, combining the ancient vedic system of learning with the modern technology, helping children to flower without repression, fear or peer pressure

- **Corporate Meditation Programs:** Specially designed and conducted in corporate firms worldwide including Microsoft, AT&T, Qualcomm, JP Morgan, Petrobras, Pepsi, Oracle, American Association of Physicians of Indian Origin (AAPI) – with focus on intuitive management, leadership skills and team work

- **Nithyananda Institute of Teachers' Training:** Over 300 teachers trained to teach: transformational meditation programs, Quantum Memory Program, Nithya Yoga, Health and Healing Programs, Spiritual Practice Programs and more

- **Media:** Articles in national and international newspapers and magazines, carrying transforming messages from Nithyananda

144

- **Nithyananda Publishers:** Over 5000 hours of Paramahamsa Nithyananda's discourses transcribed, edited and published in-house and made available in stores through books, DVDs and CDs

- **Life Bliss Gallerias:** Worldwide stores and mobile shops retailing books of Nithyananda's discourses in 23 languages and recordings of Nithya Kirtans

- **Nithyananda Meditation & Healing Centers:** Worldwide, offering meditation and healing services

- **Nithyananda Sangeeth Academy:** Music, dance and other forms of art taught and encouraged in youth and elderly alike - live and through Internet

- **Free Discourses on YouTube:** Approximately 2000 FREE discourses on www.youtube.com/lifeblissfoundation – wisdom from the master, easily accessible. Ranked top in viewership

- **Support to scientists and researchers:** Continually bridging gaps between science and spirituality through researches on spiritual energy and healing

- **Nithyananda International Youth Foundation (NIYF):** A collection of inspired youth, building a divine and dynamic society with a common ideology of peace and enlightenment

- **Women's Empowerment (WE):** A dynamic group of women with the common ideology of living enlightenment, serving society at the physical, mental and spiritual levels

- **Nithya Dheera Seva Sena:** Through transformation of self, this volunteer force of Ananda Sevaks trains and functions in the service of humanity, also serving as relief wing working towards disaster recovery management

CONTACT US

USA

Los Angeles
Nithyananda Vedic Temple,
9720 Central Avenue,
Montclair, CA 91763
Ph.: +1 909 625 1400
URL: www.NithyanandaVedicTemple.org
E mail: programs@lifeblissfoundation.org,
shop@lifebliss.org

Seattle
Nithyananda Vedic Temple,
2877, 152nd Ave NE, Bldg #13,
Redmond, WA
Ph.: +1 425 749 7073
URL: www.vedictempleseattle.org

Columbus, Ohio
Nithyananda Vedic Temple,
820 Pollock Rd,
Delaware, OH - 43015
URL: www.vedictempleohio.org

San Jose
Nithyananda Vedic Temple,
513, Los Coches Street,
Milpitas, CA – 95035
Ph.: +1 408 263 6375
URL: www.vedictemplebayarea.org
Email: info.vedictemple@gmail.com

Phoenix
Nithyananda Vedic Temple,
6605 S 39th Ave
Phoenix, AZ 85041
Ph.: +1 602 268 0233
URL: http://vedictemplephoenix.org/
Email: VedicTemplePhx@gmail.com

INDIA

Bengaluru, Karnataka
Nithyananda Dhyanapeetam,
Nithyanandapuri, Kallugopahalli,
Off Mysore Road, Bidadi – 562109
Ramnagara District, Karnataka, INDIA
Ph.: +91 80 2720 2084 / +91 97422 03311
URL: http://nithyananda.org/ashram
Email: wc@nithyananda.org

Hyderabad, Andhra Pradesh
Nithyananda Dhyanapeetam,
Nithyananda Giri, Pashambanda Sathamarai Village,
Shamshabad Mandal,
Rangareddy District – 501218
Ph.: +91 98665 00350, +91 93964 82358
URL: www.dhyanapeetam.org/web/ap
Email: dhyanapeetamhyd@gmail.com

Tiruvannamalai, Tamil Nadu
Nithyananda Dhyanapeetam,
Nithyanandapuri, Girivala path, Adiannamalai
Tiruvannamalai – 606 604
Tamilnadu, INDIA
Ph.: +91 41752 37666, +91 94449 91089
URL: http://arunachala.nithyananda.org/
Email: tvmalai@nithyananda.org

MALAYSIA

Nithyananda Dhyanapeetam Malaysia,
14, Jalan Desa Gombak 5,
Taman Desa Gombak,
53000 Kuala Lumpur, MALAYSIA
Ph.: +601 7886 1644 / +601 2235 0567
Email: nithya.nirantarananda@gmail.com

For further information visit www.nithyananda.org

EN GALLERIA

A wide range of products for blissful living:
- Nithyananda's insightful messages on video, audio tapes, CDs and books
- Enlivening music and chants for meditation and inner healing
- Meditation and yoga books, kits and CDs for rejuvenating body, mind and spirit
- Energized rosaries, bracelets, photographs, clothing and gift items for a stimulating life style
- Ethnic energy bead jewellery for men and women for tranquillity and continued high energy

Visit www.nithyanandagalleria.com or www.lifeblissgalleria.com for more information.
Email: nithyanandagalleria@gmail.com & shop@lifebliss.org

eBooks available on Amazon Kindle, Barnes & Noble, Google eBooks, Scribd, and Apple iBookstore

Follow us on
- Facebook: http://www.facebook.com/eNPublishers/
- Twitter: http://twitter.com/eNPublishers/
- WordPress: https://enpublishers.wordpress.com/

Approximately 2000 FREE discourses of Nithyananda available at YouTube: http://www.youtube.com/lifeblissfoundation/

Made in the USA
San Bernardino, CA
23 June 2019